The
Baseball Research
Handbook

The
Baseball Research
Handbook

Gerald Tomlinson

Preface by John Thorn

Society for American Baseball Research, Inc. • 1987

CONTRIBUTORS TO
The Baseball Research Handbook

Robert F. Bluthardt
Everett L. Cope
L. Robert Davids
Bill Deane
W.F. Gustafson
Stanley Grosshandler
William S. Haber
Thomas R. Heitz
Robert Hoie
Tom Jozwik
Clifford Kachline
Joseph Lawler

E. Vernon Luse
Ronald A. Mayer
Robert C. McConnell
Eugene C. Murdock
Joseph M. Overfield
John Pardon
Frank V. Phelps
David L. Porter
Dan Rappoport
Mark Rucker
Howard O. Sweet
David Q. Voigt

Contents

Preface

There may be no royal road to learning, in baseball or in anything, but who would not prefer to set out on so serpentine a journey with a clear road map and a good firm push in the right direction? While some aspects of life can certainly be learned only through first-hand experience — which often as not means first-hand mistakes — much else may be taken on authority, which rises and resides upon the mistakes of others.

Oh, to have had this invaluable little book fifteen years ago, when I first contemplated writing about baseball! Oh, the errors — of omission and commission — that would have been saved! And oh, the price I would have paid for such a guide along the researcher's path between paradise and perdition!

But you, fortunate traveler, have as your Virgil (Rome's poet, not Atlanta's catcher) the estimable Gerald Tomlinson. With this experienced writer, editor, and sleuth by your side you may traipse unafraid through the bowels of the interlibrary loan system, stride confidently to the door of Cooperstown's National Baseball Library, and even dare to write up your findings for publication.

In the years since its founding in 1971, the Society for American Baseball Research has done more to advance the study of our national pastime, through its research committees and diverse publications, than even its sixteen founders might have dreamed. SABR has issued annuals — the venerable *Baseball Research Journal*, the large-format *National Pastime*, the new *SABR Review of*

Books — and a variety of special studies, from *Great Hitting Pitchers* to *Green Cathedrals*. But as one who has been involved with many of these publications over the years, let me say that never before has the Society published so broadly **useful** a work as this. *The Baseball Research Handbook* bodes to create new researchers within SABR's current membership and to expand that membership to welcome new researchers. Thanks to Mr. Tomlinson and his distinguished band of contributors, novice researchers will produce finds more rapidly (and present them more readably) while veterans will pick up tips that will speed their labors and freshen their views. I challenge anyone in SABR to read this unassuming little book and assert he has learned nothing new.

If all this sounds a bit like the pitch of a panacea peddler (gives youth the wisdom of age, the aged the vigor of youth, and cures whatever ails), rest assured that, good as this handbook is, it will neither supply nor supplant that need for curiosity, initiative, intelligence, and luck. Mix in these, apply what you've gathered from this handbook, match them to a good topic, and set out on the road to baseball knowledge, where you'll soon join ranks with researchers like Bob Davids, Vern Luse, Frank Phelps, and Jerry Tomlinson.

CHAPTER 1

Eight Keys
to Good Research

In research, as in most other activities, there are no shortcuts to success, no magic formulas. There are some useful points to keep in mind, however, of which the following eight are fundamental.

Break New Ground

The usual reason for doing research is to make an original contribution to knowledge about a particular subject. If a topic has already been thoroughly explored — Joe DiMaggio's 56-game hitting streak in 1941, for example — there is probably no need to research it further. Of course, if you are quite sure you have, or can come up with, solid evidence for an entirely different truth than the one now accepted, then you might decide to go ahead and pursue it. What you don't want to do, though, is merely to repeat, in a different way or in different words, what most well-informed baseball fans already know.

Some new topics are inherently more significant than others. Research into the question of whether Ty Cobb or Nap Lajoie won the 1910 American League batting title is significant; indeed, in 1981 it made sports-page headlines across the nation. Research into the history of the failed Class D Anthracite League of 1928, on the other hand, will receive no such publicity. Yet both projects are original, and in their particular fields, valuable. Anything that adds to readers' understanding or knowledge of the game is worthwhile. Recognize, however, that the chances of your research being published are greater (self-publishing excepted) if your topic is of widespread interest.

Zero In

A good research topic has to be focused. That may sound rather like high-school textbook advice, but it's the simple truth. You can't explore the entire universe of baseball. The topic of "baseball" is broader than the North American continent and as varied as *Aaron to Zuverink*. You have to decide exactly what area of it you intend to research.

Your topic may be broad; it may be narrow. Are you going to produce a comprehensive three-volume history such as David Q. Voigt's *American Baseball;* or is your goal more modest, something more along the lines of Charles W. Bevis's amusing two-page piece, "Lifetime 1.000 Hitters," in the 1985 *Baseball Research Journal*? Both are focused, but their scope is quite different.

There is no mystery about what a focused topic is. Focused topics can be found everywhere. Published books on baseball, with rare exceptions, have well-defined coverage. A glance through an issue of *Baseball Research Journal* or *The National Pastime* will reveal a host of focused topics for brief articles. In fact, you won't see much in print that isn't clearly focused, because zeroing in on a topic — concentrating on a fixed field with clear boundaries — is almost always essential to publication.

Plan Where You're Going

Among writers of fiction, the argument over whether to outline or not to outline has raged for a long time. But among writers of nonfiction — particularly nonfiction that requires extensive research — there is no such argument. A good outline is a big plus and is often a necessity.

An outline doesn't necessarily have to follow the classic text-book pattern, the rigid alternation of numerals and letters, although some do. Eugene C. Murdock's superb biography of American League founder Ban Johnson was developed from a full-scale traditional outline. For a book like Murdock's, there is no substitute for detailed outlining. This doesn't mean that such an outline is cast in bronze. Far from it. The outline changes as the work progresses. An outline is a flexible working plan, not a straitjacket.

For a short article, the outline can be informal, even sketchy. Hastily scrawled notes (assuming they are based on somewhat less hasty thought) may be enough. The important thing is to have an organizing scheme in mind and to get it down on paper. Any plan is better than no plan.

Make Sure the Sources Exist

Graduate students can often tell horror stories about long-term research that has been tearfully abandoned because the crucial information couldn't be found. It sometimes happens in baseball research, too, even with experienced researchers at work on major league topics.

The problem is more acute at the minor league level. To take an example: A member of the research team for *Minor League Baseball Stars II*, Walter Kuczwara, tried vainly to find slugger Joe Munson's RBI totals in the Western League from 1927 to 1929. He never found them. Nobody else will find them either, if, as it appears, there are no such records and no accurate way to reconstruct them.

Unfortunately, the absence of sources is a danger that is easier to state than to avoid. You may not know that the sources don't exist until you have spent a great deal of time failing to find them. One of the perils of research is that the critical box score may truly be lost forever, the sought-after scrapbook may have gone up in a fire.

On the other hand, one of the thrills of research is the uncertainness of the chase, the challenge of pursuit. But an impossible challenge is seldom enjoyable. Abundant sources tend to be more comforting than a lack of sources. Too many dead ends can turn one's thoughts away from research and toward watching reruns on TV.

Find Everything You Can

The word *search* is three fourths of the word *research,* and a researcher's need to search cannot be emphasized too strongly. You want to find out everything you can about your topic. That means digging. At first, especially if you find very little material, you may conclude that not much is available. In some cases, as already noted, you will be right, but more often a thorough search will yield unexpected sources. You may even find that your topic is a kind of benign Pandora's box. Once you open up the box, the sources come flying out.

When I started to research my article "Lefty George: The Durable Duke of York," I expected the sources to be mainly small-city newspaper articles from Lefty's years on the mound. He was a minor league pitcher for most of his career, and he had died more than 25 years earlier. I had no initial inkling that a booklet had been published about this hardy pitcher (*50 Years in Baseball with Lefty George,* York, Pa., 1954) and certainly none that I might receive as a gift from his daughter, Virginia, a large carton of clippings, letters, and photos from Lefty George's own collection. One thing led to another, and the microfilm of the old and excellent *York Dispatch* proved to be just one source among many.

Be Careful!

In one way or another, every contributor to this book mentioned the need for accuracy. "I like your idea of devoting an entire

14

chapter to accuracy,' wrote Robert McConnell. "This can't be overstressed." Eugene Murdock observed, "The writer must get his facts straight." And Robert Hoie added, "I don't think you can overemphasize 'getting it right.' "

Although getting it right is the essence of research, that task can be very tough. Newspaper typos are common, and factual errors abound in baseball reporting. A harried sportswriter, working under a pressing deadline, makes a careless and, to him, not very significant mistake. The mistake is then picked up by other writers and later by baseball researchers. Although repeated *ad infinitum*, the slip-up is just as much an error as it was on the day it was made.

Richard Altick in his book *The Scholar Adventurers* makes the point that there is no major figure in history — he is talking about literary figures — "whose biography has been innocent of false-hoods and half-truths, placed there by an early memoirist and then uncritically repeated from writer to writer — and usually embroid-ered in the transmission — until at last they are disproved by the researcher." The same is true of baseball stars.

On the other hand, instead of all sources agreeing on an untruth, two sources may disagree on what should be a matter of cold fact. Or three sources may disagree. Or four. The more research you do, the more amazed you will become at the amount of misinformation that has found its way into print. It's your job as a researcher to uncover the truth, to reconcile the conflicting reports, to make your own sound judgment from the best evidence available. It's quite a job.

Keep Exact Records

Most researchers have fallen into the carelessness trap. You prob-ably will, too, sooner or later. Your notes are perfect, or seem to be, but where in the world did that fascinating bit of information come from? You have the facts down in black and white in your own handwriting. The facts are indisputable, you think, not to mention revolutionary, and they cry out to be used. But the source — "There *had* to be a source," you tell yourself — is missing. You must have that source. It's your proof, your evidence.

This does not mean that for a brief article you have to keep an elaborate set of note cards. Your research is not intended to earn you an advanced academic degree. Still, you ought to know where each item of information in your manuscript came from. If the editor says, "Prove it," you should be able to do so. Proving it does not necessarily demand a bulging card file. It may mean nothing more than having a photocopy of a box score, a clipping from a newspaper, a page reference to a *Sports Illustrated* article, a re-corded quote from an interview — anything that shows you have an actual, verifiable source and not just a guess or a recollection.

Get It Down on Paper

Somerset Maugham once wrote a short story about a man who spends most of his life assembling notes for what he believes will be a monumental work. The man grows older and older. His notes pile up higher and higher. He dies, never having gotten a word on paper.

To a dedicated researcher, that story may seem to be more like truth than fiction. It is easy, and even defensible, to defer writing until every last detail has been tracked to earth. It is especially easy if the researcher feels uneasy (or possibly terrified) about the process of writing. For many researchers, finding facts is fun; presenting them clearly on paper is work.

Writing, after all, *is* work, a special and demanding kind of work, just as playing shortstop is a special and demanding kind of work, and some people can do it better than others. No amount of effort, and surely no handbook of instruction, will turn a nonwriter into a Roger Angell or an Ed Linn. Researching and writing are two different skills. Not every outstanding researcher is an equally fine writer, although mastery of writing does give the researcher a great advantage. For one thing, it helps to make careful research accessible to a larger public, as witness Jules Tygiel's recent book on Jackie Robinson.

Still, there will always be researchers who do *not* want to write, and for those researchers the last chapter of this book provides a few hints drawn from the experience of long-time SABR editors and researchers.

CHAPTER 2
How Do I Start?

Anyone can do research. This is not to say that the job is easy or the pitfalls are nothing more than mirages. Doing first-rate research is exacting, to be sure, but not so burdensome that it requires you to abandon your means of livelihood or move within walking distance of a major library. Research sources in our information society are widely accessible. You just have to know where to look.

A Word on Libraries

A number of librarians are among SABR's best researchers, and no wonder. Generally speaking, libraries are where the research facilities and the research sources are. A librarian works in the midst of all this researcher's gold. Willie Sutton robbed banks because, as he said, "That's where the money is." If Sutton had been a baseball researcher, he would have robbed libraries — or, being a better citizen, would have simply used them.

People are sometimes intimidated by libraries, but there is no reason to be. Libraries are established and maintained to serve people, to serve *you*. No one will make that point more strongly than a professional librarian. You should resolve to make full use of a library when you work there, whether you are using your local library, a nearby college or university library, or a great research library, such as the Library of Congress or the New York Public Library.

Librarians will help you all they can. If there is one shining exception to bureaucratic apathy in the United States, it can be found in America's public libraries. But — and it is an important but — librarians can do only so much. Their job is not precisely your job. For instance:

- They cannot do your research for you. They can help you find the sources you need. They can suggest paths that you may not have considered. They can help you in countless other ways. But you must not expect them to do line-by-line investigative work for you.

- They cannot answer vague or open-ended questions. A librarian is a generalist. He or she does not know as much about Tommy Henrich, say, as you do. Your questions have to be specific. If you know that Henrich hit a memorable home run against the Brooklyn Dodgers on October 5, 1949, in Yankee Stadium, and you want more information about it, then the librarian has something specific to go on and can probably help you. If you ask the librarian to identify Tommy Henrich's finest hour as a Yankee, you have posed the wrong question. You're the one who has to find that out.

- They cannot read your mind. You should state your request in such a way that it reveals rather than disguises your intent. If you ask a librarian, "Do you have a book about Philadelphia's Baker Bowl?" the answer is going to be "No." There is no such book. But if that isn't your real question — if your real question is "How can I find details about the World Series game at Baker Bowl in 1915 when Grover Cleveland Alexander pitched the Phillies to a 3-1 win over the Boston Red Sox?" — then the librarian has a different, and promising, path to follow. Precise questions will bring you the kind of answers you need.

Your Local Library

Local libraries vary. If you live on Fifth Avenue and 65th Street in New York City, your local library is the New York Public, with its multi-million-book collection, a library that has been called "the diary of the human race." Even nearer to you at that posh address is the Donnell Library, a branch of the New York Public, but a branch of impressive size and scope.

If you live in Richmond, Virginia, on the other hand, your local library, the Richmond Public, is more modest, but a major library all the same. If you live in Corsicana, Texas, or Coos Bay, Oregon, or any of countless other places in the United States or Canada, your public library is considerably smaller. It may be a fine public library for the size of the community, but it inevitably lacks some of the sources and services of larger libraries.

Yet *any* local library, whatever its size, should ordinarily be your first stop as a baseball researcher. Your local library can get you started. It can put you on the right track. No matter how small or underfunded it may be, the library down the street can open doors on the world. In the nature of such things, some local libraries will do it better than others, but all of them can do it to some extent.

General Reference Books

Every public library has a collection of general, nonbaseball reference books that may prove helpful. At a minimum, the library should have the following references, although it may have only recent or selected volumes:

Readers' Guide to Periodical Literature
Subject Guide to Books in Print
Current Biography

A local library will also have various encyclopedias, atlases, and almanacs. A few good general reference books can often lead you to a host of special sources. Useful general references, including the three listed above, are discussed in greater detail in the next chapter.

Look in the reference section for books specifically on baseball. At a rock-bottom minimum, it should have a recent edition of *The*

Baseball Encyclopedia, published by Macmillan. Then look at the library's baseball collection, which you will find principally in Dewey Decimal section 796.357. In a large library, the reference books and general collection can be valuable for early research. In a small library, the baseball materials may not amount to much, but, even if they don't, some of the better books may list sources that will lead you to other sources.

Local Newspapers and Microfilm

Nearly all libraries have a file of local newspapers (or the local newspaper). Only a few large-city newspapers such as *The New York Times* and the *Washington Post* are thoroughly indexed, although some libraries (the Providence, Rhode Island, Public Library is one) maintain card-file indexes for the local newspaper. This system tends to be limited, but it is better than no indexing. In many cases you will know the year or even the exact date of the newspaper you need, so there's no problem. But if you do have to search for the right date, remember that since the same news story occurs on the same day everywhere, *The New York Times Index* may be all you need to find the specific date in *any* newspaper.

Back-issue newspapers in large cities and many small cities are now on microfilm. However, if either the library or the city is small and lacks microfilm readers, the newspapers you request and receive will be the real thing — old, newsprint issues just as they came off press. John Pardon tells about going through the 1946 issues of the Peekskill, New York, *Evening Star,* while researching pitcher Tony Napoles' 22-0 season in the Class D North Atlantic League. "Old newspapers can give you a tremendous feel for the times," he says. "That was important to me in doing this article, because I wanted to convey the atmosphere of that exciting postwar year."

In a larger library, one with microfilm readers, the local newspaper or newspapers from years past are likely to be available only on reels of microfilm. This makes a lot of sense, because newsprint does not stand up well to time and handling. Microfilm does. Much baseball research today relies heavily on microfilmed copies of newspapers and other periodicals.

If you live in a large city like Baltimore, it will hardly surprise you to learn that you can find the *Sun* as well as a few other, now-defunct Baltimore newspapers on microfilm at the Enoch Pratt Free Library, along with plenty of excellent machines for reading them. The famed Orioles of both the major and minor leagues have been well reported and their exploits well preserved.

The libraries in other major-league cities also offer microfilmed newspapers and imposing rows of microfilm readers. But what about the smaller cities? The cities in the minors? Well, take Macon, Georgia, home of the Pirates (once, more happily, called the Peaches). At the Washington Memorial Library in Macon you can find on microfilm any issue you may need of the Macon *Telegraph.*

How do you find out about the location and availability of microfilmed newspapers? The standard source for this kind of information is a reference work called *Newspapers in Microform,* now in its eighth edition, available at most libraries. My own source on Macon, though, was one of SABR's early publications (now out of print), Jerry Jackson's *Microfilm Index of Minor League Baseball Cities,* which is excerpted from the standard reference work.

One important point: Just as you shouldn't be intimidated by large libraries, neither should you be intimidated by microfilm or microfilm readers. They're in the library for your use, not to frighten you away. You don't have to be an audiovisual expert to do research with microfilm. Tell your librarian exactly what dates and what newspapers you're looking for. If you're unfamiliar with microfilm readers, ask the librarian to help you get the machine working. It isn't difficult. With minimal practice, you will soon feel as comfortable at a table reading microfilm as you do at a picnic taking snapshots.

Incidentally, your local librarian may have the newspapers of larger, nearby cities as well. But whether your library has the newspapers you need or not, there is another option. You can use the interlibrary loan system.

Interlibrary Loans

If your library participates in the interlibrary loan system (ILL), your potential research activities are almost limitless. This is of vital importance to a researcher who lives some distance from a major library. Your library can borrow whatever materials you need (an astonishing array of books, journals, records, and microfilm) from any participating library in the system. Your librarian will make the necessary arrangements for borrowing and will call you when the materials arrive.

There are a few points to keep in mind about the interlibrary loan system:

- Your library must be a participant in ILL.

- You must have a card at the library where you ask to do the borrowing. You can't just walk in off the street.

- Don't expect ILL libraries to lend everything. For instance, you probably won't get current reference books, very recent titles, very old or rare books, or magazines. In the case of magazines, though, you may be able to get photocopies of specific articles.

- Since most ILL operations are now computerized, you don't have to know what library has the particular item you need. The computer will track it down.

- If you borrow microfilm, your library must have a microfilm reader so that you can view it. Ideally, one or more of the machines will allow you to photocopy important pages or parts of pages, usually for a dime a copy.

- Unlike books, borrowed microfilm reels cannot be taken

home with you. They have to remain at the borrowing library for the duration of the loan.

Virtually any needed book can be borrowed. You will have to wait — usually a week to two weeks, sometimes more — for delivery of the materials to your library. But if you need a particular item, the wait is surely worth it. One reference librarian calls the interlibrary loan system "an unparalleled, bottomless pit of research wealth."

Only a limited number of libraries maintain and loan microfilm. The references already mentioned, *Newspapers on Microform* and *Microfilm Index of Minor League Baseball Cities*, list the names and dates of newspapers that are available and also show where the microfilm is located. Again, though, you don't need to know their location, because your library's computer will do the search for you.

Sometimes you will have to use your imagination in seeking the best microfilm sources. For example, if one city's newspapers prove to have had poor baseball coverage, you may find that another city in the league had excellent coverage. In that case, you may find yourself using ILL to obtain microfilm of the latter city's newspapers in preference to those from the city on which your research is focused.

Local History Collections

Not all local history is in newspapers. Many libraries have a special section of books and other materials on local history. These may or may not be helpful, depending on your area of research. In using a local history collection, you will almost certainly find it helpful to enlist the aid of the librarian in seeking what you want.

In addition to local history collections in libraries, you should consider historical societies and historical society museums as possible sources of material. Few of them feature baseball collections per se (only five such collections are listed in *The Official*

24

Museum Directory, 1987), but many historical societies — notably those of New York and Chicago — have some baseball items that they have accumulated over the years. These items may be just what you need, and the only way to find out is to check.

Three Special Libraries

In his introduction to SABR's *Green Cathedrals,* Philip J. Lowry writes that his research on ballparks took him "to both league offices, the Baseball Hall of Fame, the Negro Baseball Hall of History in Ashland, Kentucky, and to numerous libraries over the past seven years." It also took him, his wife, and son to more ballparks than they knew existed.

That's the right way to do it, and the results show the value of the effort. But many researchers will have a more restricted itinerary. You may be among them. If so, you will still find it helpful to know about the special libraries and special baseball collections that exist throughout the United States. Here is a brief rundown.

National Baseball Library

A small but excellent library devoted entirely to baseball is a part of the Baseball Hall of Fame in Cooperstown, New York. Its name is the National Baseball Library, and it contains the world's most extensive collection of printed materials devoted exclusively to baseball. With about 7,500 books, its collection is far from complete, but it possesses some items that can be found nowhere else. For instance, it has a complete collection of major league box scores from 1876 to the present. It has a superb collection of 100,000 or so photographs of players, teams, stadiums, events, and miscellaneous baseball subjects. It has a valuable file of biographical data, including questionnaires and newspaper clippings, on thousands of major league players, managers, coaches, scouts, and umpires.

Serious academic researchers are likely to make the trek to Cooperstown at least once during the development of their baseball books. Researchers go there for a variety of other reasons, too. W.P. Kinsella went there to research the background for his novel *Shoeless Joe*. Philip Roth did the same for *The Great American Novel*. Much of the research for the recent book on Topps baseball cards was done there. In the front of the 1984 SABR publication *Days of Greatness: Providence Baseball, 1875-1885* is a note to the effect that John Thorn and Mark Rucker discovered the scrapbook on which the publication is based while doing picture research at the National Baseball Library for the 1984 pictorial issue of *The National Pastime*.

The National Baseball Library manages the Film Rental Library for Major League Baseball, which at the moment contains approximately 50 films, mostly World Series and All-Star Game highlights. A two-page Statement of Services and Collections of the National Baseball Library is available upon request. The NBL's phone number is 607-547-9988; the mailing address is: National Baseball Library, National Baseball Hall of Fame & Museum, Inc., P.O. Box 590, Cooperstown, NY 13326.

Library of Congress

Let's jump from the specialized library in Cooperstown to the most general library imaginable: the Library of Congress, the nation's library. The Library of Congress is a truly immense place, but don't let its size frighten you. Anyone who has worked there will tell you that it is remarkably easy to use. Incidentally, since the Library of Congress is not a lending library, you may have to do your work there, although some books can be sent through ILL to academic libraries.

What resources does the Library of Congress offer the baseball researcher who can spend some time in Washington, D.C.? Plenty. Joseph Puccio's "Baseball Research Resources at the Library of Congress," a four-page overview, is available through

SABR. As Puccio points out, the Library has a comprehensive collection of books, both nonfiction and fiction; an array of thousands of American newspapers back through the colonial period; many complete sets of sports periodicals, including *The Sporting News*, *Sports Illustrated*, *Baseball Digest*, and *Baseball Magazine*; two important manuscript collections relating to Branch Rickey; and baseball materials in many other formats — prints and photographs, music, motion pictures, and recorded sound. Many of their newspapers and periodicals are available on microfilm.

Specific inquiries should be directed as follows (phone numbers in parentheses):

- Books: General Reading Rooms Division (202-287-5522)

- Newspapers, periodicals: Serial and Government Publications Division (202-287-5690)

- Photographs: Prints and Photographs Division (202-287-6394)

- Music: Music Division (202-287-6394)

- Movies, recordings: Motion Picture, Broadcasting and Recorded Sound Division (202-287-1000)

To write for information, address your letter to the appropriate division: Library of Congress, Washington, D.C. 20540.

Genealogical Library

If your field of interest is biographical research, you will use a variety of sources. William F. Gustafson lists and describes many of these in his article, "Locating the Old-Time Players," *Baseball Research Journal, 1973*. The next chapter of this book deals with such sources. One of those that Gustafson mentions is genealogical records. Just as there is a special baseball library, so is there a special genealogical library — the Genealogical Library of The

Church of Jesus Christ of Latter-Day Saints (Mormons) in Salt Lake City, Utah. This Genealogical Library, which is open to the public, contains the world's largest and most complete collection of genealogical information. Branch libraries throughout the United States — 650 of them — have catalogs that list the main library's holdings. Most of the main library's research materials can be obtained through the branches.

The Genealogical Library provides a brief description of its services upon request. A list of the addresses of branches is also available. One important point: The library does not usually collect records later than 1910. For records after 1910, you will find that state, county, and city offices are better sources.

To get in touch with the main library, phone 801-531-2331, or write: Genealogical Library, Church of Jesus Christ of Latter-Day Saints, 35 North West Temple Street, Salt Lake City, Utah 84150.

Although the Genealogical Library in Salt Lake City has been emphasized here, its collection is by no means the only extensive source of American genealogical materials. Other large genealogy and local history collections are those at the Fort Wayne, Indiana, Public Library; the Library of Congress and the DAR Library (Daughters of the American Revolution), both in Washington, D.C.; the New England Historic and Genealogical Society in Boston; and the New York Public Library. The most extensive in-print reference to genealogical methods and sources is *The Source: A Guidebook of American Genealogy*, edited by Arlene H. Eakle and Johni Cerny (1984).

Other Useful Collections

One of the important principles of baseball research is this: You can find sources everywhere. There are a number of specific collections (other than those in public libraries, college and university libraries, and special libraries) that should be mentioned.

Special Collections in Libraries

Most larger libraries have a reference book called *Subject Collections* by Lee Ash, published by R.R. Bowker. Although this book hardly ever becomes outdated, a new edition appears every five to seven years. Gale Research publishes a similar directory, Brigitte Darnay's *Directory of Special Libraries and Information Centers,* now in its ninth edition.

Here is a consolidated list of the libraries noted in these two directories (not repeating the libraries already described).

- **Boston Public Library,** Print Collection, Dartmouth Street at Copley Square, Boston, MA 02117: McGreevey Baseball Collection of 225 photos and paintings from the period 1870-1914.

- **Cleveland Public Library,** Social Sciences Department, 325 Superior Avenue, Cleveland, OH 44114: Charles W. Mears Baseball Collection of scrapbooks and records.

- **Detroit Public Library,** Burton Historical Collection, 5201 Woodward Avenue, Detroit, MI 48202: Ernie Harwell Collection; emphasis on the Detroit Tigers.

- **New York Public Library,** General Research Division, Fifth Avenue and 42nd Street, New York, NY 10018: A.G. Spalding Baseball Collection; Leonard Goughton Collection; also an exceptionally large general collection of baseball books and other materials, some cataloged only in the Rare Books and Manuscripts Division.

- **Pettigrew Museum Library,** Siouxland Heritage Museums, 131 North Duluth Avenue, Sioux Falls, SD 57104: Collection of Northern League Baseball Records.

- **Smithsonian Institution Libraries,** National Museum of American History Branch, Constitution Avenue at Tenth Street NW, Washington, D.C. 20560: Collection includes some 2,000 baseball cards from cigarette and chewing gum packets.

SABR's Resources

Up to this point, the emphasis on where to look has been on libraries — on where to pursue research after you have exhausted the possibilities of the materials you may own yourself. One obvious place to look is SABR. This poses something of a problem, however, since SABR has not yet established a home for its varied and increasing collections. A permanent SABR library has been under discussion for some time, but so far only the SABR Microfilm Lending Library is available to researchers.

The SABR Microfilm Lending Library is managed by member Tom Heitz, Librarian of the National Baseball Library in Cooperstown. SABR members may borrow one reel of microfilm at a time for a three-week period. Information and procedures for borrowing microfilm, along with descriptions and order forms for specific reels, are available from SABR Microfilm Library, P.O. Box 1010, Cooperstown, NY 13326 Attn: Tom Heitz, Librarian.

Here are SABR's present holdings:

- **The Sporting News.** 34 reels covering the period March 17, 1886, to December 31, 1942.

- **Sporting Life.** 29 reels covering the period April 15, 1883, through February 24, 1917.

- **Albert Spalding Baseball Collection.** 14 reels, of which four are Henry Chadwick Scrapbooks, four are Henry Chadwick Diaries, two are Harry Wright Correspondence (1878-1885), two are Knickerbocker Base Ball Club Books (1845-1868), one is Albert Spalding Scrapbooks, and one is Cincinnati Red Stockings Scorebooks (1868-1870).

Governments, Colleges, and Individuals

The kind of research you do determines in large part the kind of sources you need. If you are researching the life of Roger Maris, for example, your range of sources will be broader than — and very different from — the sources needed by a researcher doing a comparative statistical analysis of leading base stealers. Biographical research, in particular, requires going beyond purely baseball sources. You may have to write, phone, or visit government offices, such as a county recorder's office or hall of records. You may have to, or want to, interview the person whose life you are researching, or perhaps talk to his teammates, friends, relatives, or neighbors. Here is a list of places you might visit in your research. (Like libraries, these are general repositories of information, not specific sources in themselves.)

- **Town halls, courthouses, state archives.** Ordinarily, this implies a search for death certificates and the kind of information they can provide, such as the full name of deceased, date and place of birth, names of father and mother, and place of burial. Addresses for these offices can be found in *Where to Write for Vital Records: Births, Deaths, Marriages, and Divorces,* DHHS Publication No. (PHS) 84-1142, which you can buy for $1.50 from the Superintendent of Documents, U.S. Government Printing Office, Washington, D.C. 20402.

- **Colleges and universities.** Don't overlook college and university libraries in your search for sources. Some of them have excellent collections. Also, if you are doing biographical research and know that your subject attended a college or university, you may get assistance from the institution's alumni office, athletic department, or library special collections.

- **Address lists.** For major leaguers, past and present, the most convenient single source is Jack Smalling and Dennis W.

Eckes' *The Sport Americana Baseball Address List, Number 4*, published by Edgewater Book Company, Box 40238, Cleveland, OH 44140, and priced at $9.95 in paperback. For minor leaguers, there is no general list, but specific addresses may be available from the National Association of Professional Baseball Leagues, P.O. Box A, St. Petersburg, FL 33731 (813-822-6937).

● **Individuals.** When most people think of research, they think of libraries and books and microfilm readers. But some kinds of baseball research can also be done in person (or by telephone or letter) with ex-players, managers, front-office personnel, coaches, umpires, and so on. These people may have scrapbooks, clippings, photos, or other memorabilia — and they definitely will have memories. If you can't find the person you want in one of the address lists noted above, don't be discouraged. You may find the person (or a relative) listed in a telephone directory. Most local libraries and many phone companies have out-of-town telephone directories.

If all else fails, you may want to see if the editor of an appropriate newspaper or magazine will insert your query in the letters-to-the-editor column or classified ad section. You may have seen such requests for information in the *SABR Bulletin*. In some kinds of research you may find that the audience provided by a local newspaper or a ballclub fan magazine will be productive. One possible danger, depending on the nature of your project, is that too many volunteers will come forth with familiar and therefore unhelpful material. A careful wording of your request can help you to avoid that difficulty.

Asking for Information

Regardless of where you seek information, you will find these four guidelines worth keeping in mind:

1. **Be prepared.** The motto of the Boy Scouts should be your research motto. Do your homework. Learn as much as you can about your subject *before* asking a librarian for help. That way you will avoid asking questions to which you should already have found the answers — basic questions that *The Baseball Encyclopedia* or *The Complete Baseball Record Book* or even a knowledgeable fan might be able to supply.

2. **Start locally.** Just because your research involves a distant city, don't assume that you have to fly, phone, or write to a person or an institution in that city in order to gather material. First find out how much you can learn about your subject at your local library. Venture farther afield only after you have exhausted the source, including, if necessary, interlibrary loans of books and microfilmed copies of newspapers and periodicals.

3. **Ask precise questions.** Just as you must focus the research topic itself, so must you focus the individual questions you ask about it. Don't ask a librarian simple, general questions ("What do you have on the Houston Astros?") that the card catalog could easily answer. Don't make vague requests ("Please send me information on Yankee Stadium") that are open to various interpretations. Exactly what information do you want? A complete history of Yankee Stadium? An article on its restoration in 1975? A diagram of the seating arrangements? Be specific.

4. **Be courteous.** This may seem self-evident, but librarians sometimes point out that a few of the requests they receive, particularly those made by mail, are brusque and irritating. When you write for information (or when you phone, for that matter), pay attention to the tone of your request. How would *you* react to it? Would it put you in a frame of mind to make an effort to help? Or would it make you want to bury the request in the "answer sometime" file? While it's true that librarians are hired to provide service, it's also true that their reactions are pretty much the same as everyone else's. A pleasant request is more likely than an imperious one to bring a helpful response.

Three Basic Guidebooks

This baseball research handbook is a specialized look at one aspect of a very broad subject. A number of outstanding books exist on the general subject of research, and they are well worth examining for an overview of sources not specifically related to baseball. Here are three of the best:

Swidan, Eleanor A., *Reference Sources: A Brief Guide*. 9th ed. Baltimore: Enoch Pratt Free Library, 1987. 300 pp.

This small, selective book is a classic of its kind. It lists or comments on approximately a thousand of the most generally useful reference books, among them encyclopedias, biographical dictionaries, indexes to periodicals and newspapers, and a number of reference books on special subjects (not including baseball per se). The mention of any source in this respected booklet is a recommendation.

Horowitz, Lois, *Knowing Where to Look: The Ultimate Guide to Research*. Cincinnati: Writer's Digest Books, 1984. 436 pp.

A big, comprehensive book on reference sources, *Knowing Where to Look* gives a great deal of advice plus a host of recommended references. While the Enoch Pratt Free Library's booklet is an annotated list of sources, this much larger volume is a readable how-to book on basic research. Of necessity quite general, it is less scholarly and therefore more relevant to most baseball research than some of the standard works, such as Jacques Barzun and Henry F. Graff's *The Modern Researcher*.

Todd, Alden, *Finding Facts Fast*. Rev. ed. Berkeley, CA: Ten Speed Press, 1979. 123 pp.

An innovative and highly practical book on how to do efficient research, Todd's book is filled with timesaving hints. One reviewer noted that it "covers most imaginable ways to get information quickly."

CHAPTER 3

A Checklist
of Sources

The aim of the annotated list in this chapter is to describe briefly the most widely useful reference materials for baseball research. The list is far from exhaustive, and few if any items here will be unfamiliar to experienced researchers. Nevertheless, it should be useful even to those researchers as a quick review of basic sources. The list is very selective, and some of the items included are merely representative of their type. No adverse judgement is implied on any items that are not listed.

In General

These materials are the fundamental references for *any* library research. Once the card catalog has yielded whatever information it can — and after you have checked the baseball books in the reference section and the stacks, as well as in the biography section, if applicable — you are ready to move on to other sources. Here are a few of the most useful.

■ 1 *Subject Guide to Books in Print.* 1957-present. New York: R.R. Bowker, 1957-present.

This is a part of Bowker's annual *Books in Print* series. The annual *Subject Guide,* presently in four volumes, is organized by subject matter, as its title suggests. If you look under *Baseball* in the current edition, you will find some 400 books listed under the main heading and under such subheadings as *Biography, History,* and

Juvenile Literature. Most of the books listed should be available through interlibrary loan, if you cannot obtain them in any other way.

■ **2** *Cumulative Book Index*. 1928-present. New York: H.W. Wilson, 1933-present.

This is an annual author-subject-title index of books published in the English language anywhere in the world. All entries are in a single alphabetical list, the most complete entry being that for the author. *Cumulative Book Index* is indispensable for finding books no longer in print and consequently not listed in *Subject Guide to Books in Print* [1]. For books prior to 1928, see *The United States Catalog*, 4th ed. (H.W. Wilson, 1928), a two-volume reference that lists all books in print on January 1, 1928.

■ **3** *American Book Publishing Record Cumulative 1950-1957; 1876-1949*. New York: R.R. Bowker, 1978; 1980.

These 30 volumes — 15 volumes in each set — provide a subject matter arrangment of more than 920,000 books, compiled in part from the monthly *American Book Publishing Record* and in part from other sources such as the *National Union Catalog*. The arrangement is by Dewey Decimal Classification numbers. Volumes, 13, 14, and 15 in each set are author, title, and subject indexes respectively. Each year an *American Book Publishing Record Cumulative*, based on the monthly issues of the magazine, brings the record up to date.

■ **4** *Book Review Digest*. 1905-present. New York: H.W. Wilson, 1905-present.

Published monthly and later bound into annual volumes, *Book Review Digest* offers condensed critical opinion from reviewers about important books in all fields. A subject and title index appears in each annual volume, and a cumulative index is published every five years. See also the four-volume *Book Review Digest: Author/Title Index, 1905-1974* for a 70-year cumulative list.

Book Review Digest is well worth checking to see what reviewers had to say about the books you intend to use in your research.

■ **5** *Book Review Index.* 1965-present. Detroit: Gale Research, 1965-present.

Although *Book Review Index* lacks the helpful summaries of book reviews featured in *Book Review Digest*, it locates reviews in approximately twice as many periodicals. But you will have to take the extra step of checking out each of the desired periodicals.

■ **6** *The Readers' Guide to Periodical Literature.* 1900-present. New York: H.W. Wilson, 1905-present.

Approximately 180 well-known general-interest magazines, including *Sports Illustrated* and *Sport Magazine*, are indexed in *Readers' Guide*. Softcover issues appear once or twice a month and are later combined and bound into yearly volumes. Keep in mind that since *Readers' Guide* is a general index, it does not cover specialized sports publications. Two additional volumes called *19th Century Readers' Guide* cover the years 1890-1899.

■ **7** *Poole's Index to Periodical Literature.* 1802-1906. Vol. 1, 1802-1881. Boston: Osgood, 1882; vols. 2-6 (supplements 1-5). Boston: Houghton, 1888-1908. Reprint 6 vols. Gloucester, MA: Peter Smith, 1963.

Poole's, the only periodical index that covers most of the nineteenth century, lists articles by subject only, including entries for baseball. Although rather sketchy by *Readers' Guide* standards, this index can be helpful for pre-1900 research.

■ **8** *The New York Times Index.* 1851-present. New York: New York Times, 1913-present. (Early *Indexes* reproduced by R.R. Bowker)

A subject index to America's most complete newspaper, the *Times Index* is also useful for locating material in other newspapers, because it supplies dates the researcher may not know. Since newspapers are ordinarily a principal research source, this annual index can be highly useful.

■ **9** *Personal Name Index to The New York Times Index, 1851-1974; 1975-1984.* Verdi, NV: Roxbury Data Interface, 1976; 1986.

For biographical research this multi-volume index is a must. It makes finding individual names much easier than *The New York Times Index* itself does, because in the basic index the name you need may appear under another heading ("Obituaries," for example) or may be listed in a number of annual volumes, necessitating a volume-by-volume search.

■ **10** *Biography Index.* New York: H.W. Wilson, 1946-present.

This index covers biographical articles from about 2,000 popular and scholarly periodicals. It also indexes book-length biographies and chapters from collective biographies. The people listed in *Biography Index* come from all fields of endeavor. An index to professions and occupations at the end of each volume contains a baseball section.

■ **11** *Dictionary of American Biography.* 20 vols. plus 7 supplements. New York: Scribner, 1928-1981.

A monumental source of information on Americans no longer living, the DAB contains 17,656 articles in all. Only about 50 of the biographies deal with people who had some direct connection with baseball. See David Q. Voigt's "Baseball and the DAB" in the *Baseball Research Journal, 1976.* A forthcoming SABR Research Guide from the Bibliography Committe will update the list of DAB baseball references.

■ **12** *Current Biography.* 1940-present. New York: H.W. Wilson, 1940-present.

This monthly reference service offers readable, informative profiles of people in the news, including sports figures. Annual bound volumes appear, and the articles are well indexed and easy to locate. For a complete baseball-related index of *Current Biography*, see Joseph Lawler's *SABR Research Guide No. 1* (Bibliography Committee), 1986.

Baseball Bibliographies

Most of the remaining materials in this checklist are concerned wholly or principally with baseball, beginning with two baseball bibliographies. For a thorough and perceptive review of Smith's bibliography [13], including useful comparisons with Grobani's [14], see Frank V. Phelps, *SABR Bibliography Committee Newsletter, 87-1, February 16, 1987*, and his commentary in *The SABR Review of Books*, 1987.

■ **13** *Baseball: A Comprehensive Bibliography*. Compiled by Myron J. Smith, Jr., Jefferson, NC: McFarland & Company, 1986. 915 pp.

The largest baseball bibliography in print, Smith's compilation covers "books and monographs; scholarly papers; government documents; doctoral dissertations; masters' theses; poetry and fiction in limited amount; pro team yearbooks and other publications; college and pro All-Star Game and World Series programs; commercially produced yearbooks . . .; and periodical and journal articles, including the first-ever analysis of the diamond-oriented contents of *Baseball Magazine, Baseball Digest, Sport, Sports Illustrated,* and *Inside Sports,*" as well as articles from more than 350 other listed journals. The inclusion of many journal articles and selections from books is the great virtue of Smith's book. It excludes "book reviews, most poetry, fiction, and music, and newspaper articles (unless reprinted in nonfiction anthologies)"; it also omits citations from the so far unindexed *Sporting Life* and *The Sporting News.* Despite errors and omissions, Smith's book can be a good starting point for baseball research. But it does not replace the older Grobani [14].

■ **14** *Guide to Baseball Literature.* Edited by Anton Grobani. Detroit: Gale Research, 1975. 363 pp.

This pioneering bibliography, covering items published through 1972, contains items and categories not listed by Smith, including early club constitutions, periodicals, baseball fiction and poetry. As Frank V. Phelps points out in his Bibliography Committee review, the Grobani bibliography lists more than 800 nonfiction books and monographs, some of them well known and respected, that are missing from Smith's book. Consequently, a researcher will do well to consult both bibliographies — and not assume that the larger and more recent Smith bibliography supersedes Grobani's. Both are valuable. Both have their strengths, and both unfortunately have their definite, though different, weaknesses.

Baseball Encyclopedias

Although there are a number of baseball encyclopedias in print, only three are listed here. The first two are called encyclopedias. The third is not, but its comprehensive coverage makes it fit this category more logically than any other.

■ **15** *The Baseball Encyclopedia: The Complete and Official Record of Major League Baseball.* 6th ed. Joseph L. Reichler, Editor. New York: Macmillan, 1985. 2,750 pp.

Since the appearance of the first edition in 1969, this massive volume has probably spurred more baseball research projects than any other book. Strictly speaking, *The Baseball Encyclopedia* is more of a fact-packed records-and-statistics book than it is a typical encyclopedia. By whatever name, it is an indispensable resource. The longest parts of the encyclopedia are the alphabetically arranged player and pitcher registers — complete individual major league career records. However, the entire book is a cornucopia of facts and figures. In *The Bill James Historical Baseball Abstract,* Jim Carothers says of *The Baseball Encyclopedia* that it "marked the beginning of advanced statistical analysis of the game" and that if "the last library in the world were on fire, this is the baseball book that would be most desirable to save."

■ **16** *The Sports Encyclopedia: Baseball.* 7th ed. David S. Neft and Richard M. Cohen, Editors. New York: St. Martin's Press, 1987. 606 pp.

This encyclopedia contains a wealth of information arranged differently from that in *The Baseball Encyclopedia.* Instead of concentrating on individuals, it focuses on seasons, beginning with 1901. Nearly nine tenths of the book is organized by years, listing the teams, their finishes, rosters, and statistics. For every year in each league there is a useful narrative introduction. Despite some discrepancies in the statistics for certain star players and established regulars from those given in *The Baseball Encyclopedia* [15], this book has much to commend it. A researcher interested in complete yearly rosters and in the statistical march of baseball history since 1901 (rather than in an alphabetical list of players and managers) will find it a valuable reference.

■ **17** *All-Time Rosters of Major League Baseball Clubs.* By S.C. Thompson. Rev. ed. Revisions by Pete Palmer. New York: A.S. Barnes, 1973. 723 pp.

For complete yearly lists of all the personnel of every major league baseball club from 1876 to 1972, this is the book, although it does contain some errors for the early years. The books includes yearly records for each player, positions played, and number of games at each position. The same material can be found in other references, but not in as accessible a format.

Baseball Rules

Official rule books have been issued by many publishers. From 1920 to 1942 they were printed in detachable booklet form in the

Spalding, Reach, Spalding-Reach, and The Sporting News baseball guides. Today the rules appear in a separate booklet.

■ **18** *Official Baseball Rules.* 1950-present. St. Louis: The Sporting News, 1950-present.

The latest official rules appear in a 101-page paperback booklet, issued annually and updated, if necessary, with the year's changes underlined. The rules are organized in handbook format under major headings (e.g., 7.00 — The Runner) and subheadings (e.g., 7.06 [a specific rule]).

Collective Biographies

Assembling a group of ballplayers' biographies seems to be the sportswriter's national pastime. Myron J. Smith's *Baseball: A Comprehensive Bibliography* [13] lists 1,414 collective biographies of players, managers, owners, executives, coaches, and umpires. Many of them are good, some are outstanding, but only a few are comprehensive enough to be considered general sources.

■ **19** *Biographical Dictionary of American Sports: Baseball.* David L. Porter, Editor. Westport, CT: Greenwood Press, 1987. 736 pp.

Modeled on the *Dictionary of American Biography*, this reference volume contains biographies of 519 players, managers, executives, and umpires. The biographies, arranged alphabetically from Hank Aaron to Robin Yount, were written by 104 contributors, who did extensive research to ensure the factual accuracy of the entries and to provide anecdotes on many of the subjects.

■ **20** *Who's Who in Professional Baseball.* By Gene Karst and Martin J. Jones, Jr. New Rochelle, NY: Arlington House, 1973. 919 pp.

This book consists of brief narrative biographies, written in a telegraphic style, of more than 1,000 major league ballplayers, managers, owners, and others directly associated with baseball. The information in the sketches was obtained by interview, first-hand observation, questionnaire, magazine and newspaper files, and from the publicity directors of both major leagues and of the then twenty-four major league teams. The sketches contain highlights and anecdotes of the subjects' lives. Only cumulative lifetime stats are shown. No bibliography or references are included.

Baseball Address List

This reference was described briefly on page 31, along with its publisher's address and price.

■ **21** *The Sport Americana Baseball Address List.* No. 4. By R.J. "Jack" Smalling and Dennis W. Eckes. Cleveland: Edgewater Book Company, 1986.

Intended as an autograph hunter's guide, this paperback is useful for obtaining mailing addresses of major leaguers who are still living. Deceased players are also listed, with their date and place of death. Smalling and Eckes' alphabetical list includes virtually every player entering the major leagues since 1910. A list of major league umpires and coaches without major league playing experience, also debuting since 1910, is included as well. Earlier editions, No. 1 (1980) and No. 2 (1982), listed players debuting between 1871 and 1910.

Baseball Record Books

Publishers past and present have put out a wide variety of record books. Obviously, if record books are to be relied upon for recent information or all-time records, they must be constantly updated.

Two record books are included in this list. Both are annual publications.

■ **22** *The Complete Baseball Record Book*. Craig Carter, Editor. St. Louis: The Sporting News, 1986-present.

This large-format paperback book, 351 pages in 1987, consolidates the material in the long-standing *Baseball Dope Book, Official Baseball Record Book,* and *Official World Series Records.* Included in the new *Record Book* are all the statistics one would expect, organized by (1) regular season, (2) championship series, (3) World Series, (4) All-Star Game, then further broken down by records in batting, baserunning, pitching, and fielding. Completing the regular-season section are yearly leaders, team finishes, career milestones, and general reference data.

■ **23** *The Book of Baseball Records*. 1987 ed. Seymour Siwoff, Editor and Publisher. New York: Seymour Siwoff, 1987. 394 pp.

This record book began in 1926 as *The Little Red Book of Baseball* and has been updated by various publishers since then. In 1972, under the aegis of the Elias Sports Bureau, it took its present title. Similar to (but less complete than) TSN's *Record Book,* it is primarily a compilation of superlatives — the most, the greatest, the longest, the lowest, and the fewest, but with emphasis, too, on championship series, World Series, and All-Star records. Each section lists records in this order: lifetime, season, game, and inning.

Baseball Guides

Many commercial publishers — as well as both major leagues, most minor leagues, all major league clubs, and some minor league clubs — put out annual yearbooks, record books, media guides, and so on. Older editions of these guides are not generally available, except perhaps from personal collections, memorabilia dealers, or the National Baseball Library in Cooperstown. A few annuals are standard, well-established publications, and those are the ones listed here.

■ **24** *The Sporting News Official Baseball Guide.* 1942-present. St. Louis: The Sporting News, 1942-present.

This paperback annual, 528 pages in 1987, provides a review of the prior season in the major and minor leagues, including an overall narrative account, individual team accounts in both major leagues, detailed information on the championship series, World Series, and All-Star Game. It also has special features based on the events of the season, league leaders in various categories, award winners, obituaries, directories of the major and minor leagues, and a rundown of the season's minor league averages. For a detailed description and indexes to the feature articles and records of "Former Stars," which appeared in earlier editions, see Robert C. McConnell's *SABR Research Guide No. 3* (Bibliography Committee), 1986.

■ **25** *The Sporting News Official Baseball Register.* 1940-present. St. Louis: The Sporting News, 1940-present.

This paperback annual, 576 pages in 1987, has the same basic format as the manager, player, and pitcher registers in *The Baseball Encyclopedia.* The *Register* is an alphabetical list of all active players (including pitchers, although in earlier editions players and pitchers had separate listings), with managers' records listed in the back; editions through 1980 also supplied the playing records of coaches and selected old-timers. Each player's yearly and lifetime major league statistics are included and are updated each year. A noteworthy difference between the *Baseball Register* and *The Baseball Encyclopedia* is that the *Register* provides more personal and career information about each player and manager, including minor league stats. An older, similar paperback annual is *Who's Who in Baseball,* which first appeared in 1912, then yearly from 1916 to date, long outlasting its original sponsor, *Baseball Magazine* [46].

■ **26** *The American League Red Book.* 1937-present. New York: American League of Professional Baseball Clubs, 1937-present.

Called the *American League Rookie and Record Book* until 1943, the *Red Book* offers a wide range of statistical and personnel information for the year preceding the date on the cover. The book contains a wealth of information on each club: ballpark type, measurements, address, admission prices, manager's sketch, rosters, scouting directory, list of front-office personnel, minor league affiliations, and more. The Table of Contents gives an excellent overview of the varied contents of the book.

■ **27** *National League Green Book.* 1934-present. New York: The National League of Professional Baseball Clubs, 1934-present.

Like the *American League Red Book,* this paperback annual contains statistics, league and club data, rosters, records, and so on. The coverage is similar but not identical to that in the *Red Book.*

■ **28** *Baseball America's Baseball Directory.* 1984-present. Baseball America, 1984-present.

Although this book contains major league directories of front-office personnel and spring training information, it concentrates on baseball below the major league level. Two thirds of the book, 136 pages in 1987, deals with the minor leagues, Latin baseball, winter baseball, college and high school baseball, and summer and youth baseball. As a source of recent information on records, names, and addresses at these lower levels, the *Directory* is unsurpassed.

■ **29** *Baseball America's Baseball Statistics Report.* 1983-present. Baseball America, 1983-present.

This statistical compilation for the season preceding the date on its cover deals briefly with the majors, but, like the *Directory* above, its real value lies in its detailed coverage of the minor leagues and college baseball. For each of the minor leagues, it lists final team standings, individual batting and pitching records, department leaders in batting and pitching, and league champions since the league was founded.

Early Baseball Guides

At one time or another, most athletic equipment manufacturers have published baseball annuals. Wright & Ditson put one out from 1884 to 1886 and from 1910 to 1912. Rawlings issued one from 1922 to 1946. Perhaps the most useful guides for the researcher — spanning the history of baseball from 1860 to 1946 — are the following seven.

■ **30** *Beadle's Dime Base-Ball Player.* 1860-1881. Henry Chadwick, Editor. New York: Beadle & Co., 1860-1881.

This is the grandfather of them all, the first guide published for sale to the public. It lists records, rules, averages (beginning in 1861), noteworthy games, member clubs of and delegates to the National Association and the National League. *Beadle's* expired when Chadwick took over as editor of the more successful *Spalding's.*

■ **31** *DeWitt's Base-Ball Guide.* 1868-1885. First issue edited by M.J. Kelly; later issues edited by Henry Chadwick. New York: Robert M. DeWitt, 1868-1885.

Similar in many respects to *Beadle's* [30], this annual publication contains rules of the game, a model constitution and by-laws for ball clubs, instructions on scoring, and hints on playing, training, and umpiring. Players' averages first appeared in the 1872 edition. From 1872 to 1876 *DeWitt's* was the official publication of the Amateur and Professional Association.

■ **32** *Spalding's Official Base Ball Guide.* 1878-1939. New York: A.G. Spalding & Bros., 1878-1893; New York: American Sports Publishing Co., 1894-1939.

For more than half a century, this paperback guide was the most widely known and sold of the statistical reviews. It even went international at one point, with British, Australian, and Cuban editions. *Spalding's*, the National League's official guide, included records, averages, various other statistics, and rules. From 1908 to 1924, the *Spalding* guides contained only a brief narrative record along with team standings for each of the minor leagues. Detailed minor league records for those years appear in *Spalding's Official Base Ball Record* [33].

■ **33** *Spalding's Official Base Ball Record.* 1908-1924. New York: American Sports Publishing Co., 1908-1924.

This annual compilation lists complete individual stats of regular players in all professional leagues, including the minors, as well as a chronology of the previous season, selected information on semipro and college team records for the year, and all-time records. In 1925 and thereafter these records reappeared in the *Guide*.

■ **34** *Reach's Official Base Ball Guide.* 1883-1939. Philadelphia: A.J. Reach, 1883-1927; A.J. Reach, Wright & Ditson, 1928-1934; New York: American Sports Publishing Co., 1935-1939.

Starting as *Reach's Base Ball Guide,* this publication had a number of titles over the years, but always included the name *Reach.* Originally the official guide of the American Association, it outlived its sponsor, switched its allegiance to the American League, and became that league's official guide in 1902. Over the years, *Reach's* coverage remained similar to but somewhat more comprehensive than *Spalding's.*

■ **35** *Spalding-Reach Official Base Ball Guide.* 1940-1941. New York: American Sports Publishing Co., 1940-1941.

For two years the *Spalding's Guide* and *Reach's Guide* appeared in a consolidated edition. These were big, comprehensive books (470 + pages each year plus a detachable 64-page book of

Official Baseball Rules). The merged version gave way in 1942 to the new Sporting News *Guide* [24].

■ **36** *1943 Baseball; Official Baseball 1945-1946.* Chicago: Office of the Baseball Commissioner, 1943; New York: A.S Barnes & Co., 1945-1946.

The massive 1943 book (736 pages) is sometimes called the "Commissioner's Guide" or the "Landis Guide" because of its origin in the Commissioner's office. The Barnes books are only about half as long, even though the 1945 edition covers both 1943 and 1944. These three publications — containing complete major and minor league team and individual records, plus official rules, and, in 1943, impressive illustrations — provide a solid, comprehensive record of wartime baseball.

Current Baseball Newspapers

The sports pages of local newspapers are a prime source for many baseball researchers. There are also past and present newspapers, mostly weeklies, devoted either exclusively or in part to baseball. Here are the three main ones now being published.

■ **37** *The Sporting News.* 1886-present. St. Louis: C.C. Spink & Son; The Sporting News, 1886-present.

A weekly newspaper, *The Sporting News*, with a present circulation of about 700,000, is often called the "bible of baseball." In addition to baseball, it covers football, basketball, and hockey in considerable detail. Still, its major emphasis has always been on baseball, and its incisive reporting and excellent columns — not to mention its complete box score coverage of major league baseball — make it a must in many research projects. It also covers the minors, although less so today than in earlier years. The SABR Microfilm Lending Library owns 34 reels of *The Sporting News,* 1886-1942 (see page 30).

■ **38** *Baseball America.* 1981-present. Durham, NC: American Sports Publishing, 1981-present.

Baseball America, a newspaper in the same general format as *The Sporting News,* is published twice monthly from March through October and monthly from November through February. It has a circulation of about 10,000. The paper's motto is "Baseball News You Can't Get Anywhere Else . . ." — which originally meant heavy emphasis on the minor leagues, with some attention to college baseball, high school baseball, the winter leagues, coverage of the draft, and so on. Recently the balance has tipped a bit more toward the majors, but *Baseball America* still remains essentially a minor league counterpart, and a good one, of *The Sporting News.*

■ **39** *Baseball Bulletin.* 1976-present. Rochester, MI: Donald Publications, 1976-present.

This is a bimonthly newspaper that contains feature articles, columns, and book reviews. It concentrates on the current major league baseball scene, but it also offers some minor league coverage and a glimpse at baseball history.

Early Baseball Newspapers

Two baseball newspapers no longer published are especially worth exploring for the early history of the game. Like *The Sporting News,* these newspapers cover more than baseball, but their early coverage of the national game is excellent.

■ **40** *New York Clipper.* 1853-1924.

The *Clipper* was a weekly variety newspaper, but its coverage of baseball in the early years was extensive. David Q. Voigt in his *American Baseball: From Gentleman's Sport to the Commissoner System* quotes from the *Clipper* more frequently than from any other source.

■ **41** *Sporting Life.* Francis C. Richter, Editor. 1883-1917; 1922-1926. Name changed to *Sport Life* in 1924. Philadelphia: Sporting Life Publishing Co., 1883-1917; 1922-1926.

A weekly newspaper covering "base ball, trap shooting and general sports" according to its masthead, the breezy *Sporting Life* competed with the more staid *Sporting News* for about 30 years. So dominant was editor Richter that when he died, *Sporting Life* died as well, although it was later revived for a time. The SABR Microfilm Lending Library owns 29 reels of *Sporting Life,* 1883-1917 (see page 30).

Current Baseball Magazines

When it comes to magazines, baseball articles can turn up almost anywhere; in *Sports Illustrated* and *Sport Magazine,* naturally, but also in *People,* in *Fortune,* in the *New Yorker,* in *American Heritage,* in newsweeklies, in men's magazines, in alumni magazines, in historical society journals. Which is one reason why *Readers' Guide* [6] is so often worth consulting. It won't lead you to all magazine sources, but it will give you a good start.

Besides the general-interest magazines, there are a few periodicals whose coverage is restricted to baseball.

■ **42** *Baseball Digest.* 1942-present. Evanston, IL: Century Publishing Co., 1942-present.

More for the fan than for the student of the game, "baseball's only monthly magazine" contains a cross section of articles, some original, others reprinted from newspapers throughout the country. Profiles and players' careers get primary emphasis, but the magazine also presents analyses, rosters, and original statistical tables.

■ **43** *Baseball Research Journal.* 1972-present. Cooperstown, NY, and Kansas City, MO: Society for American Baseball Research, 1972-present.

This pioneering SABR publication began as an 80-page type-written booklet. The best articles from the first three *Journals* — 1972, 1973, and 1974 — were consolidated and published by SABR as *Baseball Historical Review* in 1981. Issues from 1975 to date are still in print. The *Journal* changed to a new, larger format in 1984. A *Baseball Research Journal Index* was published in 1982 and updated in 1987. If you intend to work on an article for the *Journal*, you may want to study prior issues (or simply go through the most recent *Index*), first to make sure that the topic hasn't already been covered, and second to get a general idea of the requirements for publication.

■ **44** *The National Pastime.* 1982-present. Cooperstown, NY, and Kansas City, MO: Society for American Baseball Research, 1982-present.

A large-format, strikingly designed and handsomely illustrated magazine that began as an annual, went to two issues in 1984, and then reverted to once a year, *The National Pastime* features outstanding baseball writing and rare photographs. Predominantly pictorial issues have appeared in 1984 and 1986.

■ **45** *Baseball History.* 1986-present. Westport, CT: Meckler Publishing Corporation, 1986-present.

This quarterly magazine is too new to qualify as a major source, but it is worth examining as a variant of SABR's *Baseball Research Journal.* Its approach is more scholarly than that of SABR's journal, with some of the articles having extensive source notes. The articles, apart from their considerable merit, can be useful to a new researcher, since the notes indicate where the author's information came from, something SABR's journal articles do not do. *Baseball History* ends with a book review section.

Another promising new publication, also established in 1986, is *The SABR Review of Books,* edited by Paul D. Adomites. Subtitled *A Forum of Baseball Literary Opinion,* this annual journal provides detailed reviews of recent baseball books and a variety of features on the literature of baseball.

Early Baseball Magazine

Among the many baseball periodicals that did not survive, one deserves special notice.

■ **46** *Baseball Magazine*. 1908-1957; 1964-1965. Boston, New York, and Washington, D.C.: Baseball Magazine Co., 1908-1957; 1964-1965.

Intended as a monthly, the magazine fell on hard times in the early 1950s, and the number of issues per year was reduced until the magazine folded. An attempted resurrection in the 1960s failed. *Baseball Magazine* offered a wide selection of articles, including profiles of ballplayers, analyses of strategy and statistics, and historical perspectives on the game.

Special SABR Publications

Research is an ongoing process. Baseball publications that are the result of research, and thus add to the knowledge of the national pastime, become in turn sources for future research. This phenomenon is not limited to SABR publications, of course, but since SABR is the leading baseball research organization in the country, and since SABR publications are exceptionally useful as research sources, four of them are listed here.

■ **47** *This Date in Baseball History*. L. Robert Davids, Editor. Cooperstown, NY: Society for American Baseball Research, 1976; revised edition, 1982. 56 pp.

The book that set the pattern for a host of commercial *This Date in . . .* books, not to mention a lot of calendars, SABR's original publication covers a century of major league baseball, beginning with April 4 (the earliest opening game) and ending with the latest World Series game (October 28).

■ **48** *Minor League Baseball Stars*, Vols. I and II. L. Robert Davids, Editor. Cooperstown, NY: Society for American Baseball

Research, 1978 (Vol. 1); 1985 (Vol. 2). 125 pp. (Vol. 1); 158 pp. (Vol. 2).

In format, these books are the minor league equivalent of the register sections of *The Baseball Encyclopedia*. Volume I has the lifetime stats of 170 outstanding minor league players. Volume II covers more than 200 additional players and managers. A third volume is planned. For research on the minors, these books are invaluable.

■ **49** *Great Hitting Pitchers.* L. Robert Davids, Editor. Cooperstown, NY: Society for American Baseball Research, 1979. 70 pp.

Evolutionary changes in hitting by pitchers are traced in this book, as are the revolutionary changes brought about by the introduction of the designated hitter in the American League. The book contains statistics on many aspects of pitchers as hitters, such as top game batting performances, annual leaders in batting average, career batting records, pitchers as pinch hitters, and AL pitchers' hitting since 1973.

■ **50** *Green Cathedrals.* By Philip J. Lowry. Cooperstown, NY: Society for American Baseball Research, 1986. 157 pp.

A large-format, illustrated paperback that presents the vital statistics for every ballpark that has ever been used for an official professional game in the major leagues and the Negro leagues. The information is presented in outline form under these headings: style, a.k.a., occupant, location, surface, dimensions, fences, former use, current use, and phenomena. Lowry spent seven years on this project and received over 2,300 letters in response to requests. The book contains an excellent bibliography.

Books from Major Publishers

A collection of all the baseball books ever put out by commercial and university-press publishers would fill several rooms. The baseball books still in print can be found, as noted earlier, in *Subject Guide to Books in Print* [1]. Many of the others can be located in *Baseball: A Comprehensive Bibliography* [13] and *Guide to Baseball Literature* [14]. Since the specific books you need for research will vary from project to project, the rest of this checklist will concentrate mainly on particular types of books, with a few representative titles given to illustrate each type.

General Histories

Two general histories of baseball deserve mention. The first is Harold Seymour's impressive two-volume study.

- **51** *Baseball: The Early Years* (to 1903). New York: Oxford University Press, 1960. 373 pp.

- **52** *Baseball: The Golden Years* (to 1930). New York: Oxford University Press, 1971. 492 pp.

The second general history is David Q. Voigt's. His three volumes provide a readable, well-documented overview.

- **53** *American Baseball: From Gentleman's Sport to the Commissioner System* (to 1920). Norman: University of Oklahoma Press, 1966. 336 pp.

- **54** *American Baseball: From the Commissioners to Continental Expansion* (to 1945). Norman: University of Oklahoma Press, 1970. 350 pp.

- **55** *American Baseball: From Postwar Expansion to the Electronic Age* (to 1982). University Park: Pennsylvania State University Press, 1983. 414 pp.

Seymour's and Voigt's books are the most complete general histories now in print, but a few fine one-volume histories of baseball were published prior to theirs.

■ 56 Spink, Alfred H., *The National Game: A History of Baseball, America's Leading Outdoor Sport, from the Time It Was First Played Up to the Present Day*. St. Louis: The National Game Publishing Co., 1910. 355 pp. A revised and enlarged second edition, with corrections by W.M. Rankin, was published in 1911. This revised edition, the preferable one, contains 410 pages and can be identified by a notation on page LXII.

■ 57 Spalding, Albert G., *America's National Game: Historic Facts Covering the Beginning, Evolution, Development, and Popularity of Baseball, with Personal Reminiscences of Its Vicissitudes, Its Victories, and Its Votaries*. New York: American Sports Publishing Co., 1911. 542 pp.

One book that is hard to classify but deserves special mention is Lawrence S. Ritter's classic work, originally published in 1966 and expanded in 1984. The book, whose subtitle tells it all, was originally based on interviews with 26 baseball greats; four more interviews were added to the 1984 edition.

■ 58 Ritter, Lawrence S., *The Glory of Their Times: The Story of the Early Days of Baseball Told by the Men Who Played It*. Rev. ed. New York: William Morrow, 1984. 368 pp. The first edition of this book, 300 pp., was published by Macmillan in 1966.

League and Team Histories

The specific sources you need will obviously depend on your project. The ones included here are excellent examples of their kind and are worth exploring as models if not as sources.

■ **59** Allen, Lee, *The National League Story*. New York: Hill & Wang, 1961. Rev. ed., 1965. 293 pp.

This is the official history of the National League through 1964, written by a former historian of the National Baseball Hall of Fame in Cooperstown. It is a good capsule history, a useful overview of the senior circuit.

■ **60** Allen, Lee, *The American League Story*. New York: Hill & Wang, 1962. 242 pp.

A companion volume to Allen's history of the National League, this book is an excellent brief review of American League history from 1901 to 1961. Like its companion, it is a solid, readable secondary source.

■ **61** Lieb, Frederick G., *The Detroit Tigers*. New York: G.P. Putnam, 1946. 276 pp.

This is one of many good team histories published by G.P. Putnam's in the 1940s and 1950s. Obviously, the history you need is the one that covers your area of interst. It may be Lee Allen's *The Cincinnati Reds* (1948), or Franklin Lewis's *The Cleveland Indians* (1949), or Harold Kaese and Russell G. Lynch's *The Milwaukee Braves* (1954). Since these are nonscholarly histories and secondary sources, without indexes, they are useful in a research sense mainly as background reading. Some recent team histories are more comprehensive, such as Art Ahrens and Eddie Gold's *The Cubs: The Complete Record of Chicago Cubs Baseball* (New York: Macmillan, 1986) and Donald Honig's *Dodgers: The Complete Record of Dodger Baseball* (New York: Macmillan, 1986).

■ **62** Asinof, Eliot, *Eight Men Out: The Black Sox and the 1919 World Series*. New York: Holt, Rinehart and Winston, 1963. 302 pp.

This is a superb account of the biggest scandal in baseball history. However, as Asinof makes clear in his preface, he has fictionalized the account for readability, supplying a considerable amount of made-up dialogue. Thus, although carefully researched and fascinating to read, the book represents what historian Barbara W. Tuchman once called "the 'he must have' style of historical writing." Asinof explains candidly and convincingly why he lacks documentary support for some of what he writes. But a researcher cannot ignore that lack.

Biographies

In a research sense, a biography is a source whose usefulness depends on your specific topic — and on the seriousness (which does not necessarily mean stuffiness) of the biographer. If the book has bibliographic notes or, better yet, a bibliographic essay, as in Eugene C. Murdock's *Ban Johnson: Czar of Baseball*, the biography may be helpful to you well beyond the subject's life story.

■ **63** Murdock, Eugene C., *Ban Johnson: Czar of Baseball*. Westport, CT: Greenwood Press, 1982. 294 pp.
A scholarly baseball biography, this life of the founder of the American League is an outstanding example of its kind. Not only is it thoroughly researched and documented, it is also well-written and entertaining. It is that rarity in baseball biography, a secondary source that a researcher can feel safe in relying on. For a good scholarly biography of a ballplayer, see Jules Tygiel's *Baseball's Great Experiment: Jackie Robinson and His Legacy* (Oxford University Press, 1983).

■ **64** Smelser, Marshall, *The Life That Ruth Built: A Biography*. New York: Quadrangle Books, 1975. 592 pp.
This is a popular biography that covers Babe Ruth's life in thorough detail. Based on nearly 2,000 news and feature stories from newspapers, it gives a good sense of how major league baseball was played during the Ruth era. Smelser, who includes a biblio-

graphy, makes a point of accepting no unsubstantiated tales of the Babe's excesses. Like most secondary sources, *The Life That Ruth Built* is mainly useful to a researcher as background reading.

■ **65** Appel, Martin, and Burt Goldblatt, *Baseball's Best: The Hall of Fame Gallery*. 2nd ed. New York: McGraw-Hill, 1980. 448 pp.

This well-illustrated collective biography is one of a number of good books on Baseball Hall of Famers. The text is detailed and excellent, although the players' stats show career totals only. Another fine collective biography is Bob Broeg's *Super Stars of Baseball* (St. Louis: The Sporting News, 1971). The Brooklyn nostalgia buff's biographical bible is Roger Kahn's *The Boys of Summer* (New York: Harper & Row, 1971).

Autobiographies

An autobiography is a primary source; it is the life story of the writer told by himself. But baseball autobiographies, like many other autobiographies, can't always be trusted. A few of them are self-serving; some make no pretense of being much more than potboilers; and most (even the best) are ghostwritten, whether or not that is made clear on the title page. You will have to exercise your critical judgment in determining how much to rely on any given baseball autobiography. Here are some especially good ones.

■ **66** Anson, Adrian C., *A Ball Player's Career*. Chicago: Era Publishing Co., 1900. 339 pp.

Cap Anson's autobiography is a fascinating personal account of the early days of baseball. The book covers his career from boyhood games in Marshalltown, Iowa, through his debut with the Rockford Forest Citys in 1871, and on through the glory days with Philadelphia and, preeminently, Chicago. A candid look at nineteenth century professional baseball, with glimpses of the great first baseman-manager's personal life apart from the game, his opinions of some of the other stars of the day, and an account of the 1889 world tour. Anson comes through as a fascinating character on and off the field.

■ **67** Robinson, Jackie, as told to Alfred Duckett, *I Never Had It Made*. New York: G.P. Putnam, 1972. 287 pp.

Jackie Robinson, unlike most ballplayers, is a significant historical figure. That hardly guarantees a worthwhile autobiography (witness those of some recent Presidents), but in fact this is an impressive one. Duckett let Robinson speak into a tape recorder and then, with a minimum of intrusion, shaped the material for publication. The events themselves are exciting; Robinson is honest and straightforward; and the result is exemplary.

■ **68** Williams, Ted, as told to John Underwood, *My Turn at Bat: The Story of My Life*. New York: Simon & Schuster, 1969. 288 pp.

This book received almost universal acclaim when it appeared: "The author has captured it all . . . like a good interviewer, Underwood lets his subject ramble." A reader gets the feeling that Williams is telling his own story — and telling it straight. The book is frank and honest, a model of its type.

■ **69** Veeck, Bill, and Ed Linn, *Veeck — as in Wreck*. New York: G.P. Putnam, 1962. 380 pp.

Bill Veeck, the irrepressible club owner who, among his various promotional stunts, signed midget Eddie Gaedel to pinch-hit for the St. Louis Browns, taped his recollections for this autobiography. Sportswriter Ed Linn then did a masterful job of putting Veeck's recollections in shape for publication. The result is one of the most highly regarded baseball books of all time, an amusing and engrossing autobiography with the ring of truth.

■ **70** Kuhn, Bowie, *Hardball: The Education of a Baseball Commissioner*. New York: Times Books, 1987. 453 pp.

A self-portrait of Bowie Kuhn's tenure as baseball commissioner from 1969 to 1984, with editorial assistance by Martin Appel, this book gives an insider's view of baseball from the top. Kuhn tells how the tough decisions of those years were made, presenting his side of the controversies that arose with Charles O. Finley, George Steinbrenner, Marvin Miller, and others. It provides an informative look at baseball during the years in which television became an ever more dominant force.

Fiction

Fiction by its very nature is not a research source. No matter how thoroughly the writer may have studied his subject or how accurately he may have presented it, fiction remains fiction. It is an excellent subject for research but not, except in and of itself, a source for it. Even when the on-field incidents are accurate and when respected authorities are cited, as in Eric Rolfe Greenberg's *The Celebrant* (New York: Everest House, 1983), no one is going to use the book for research (in this case, for the life of Christy Mathewson). Most baseball novels are frankly fictional. Bernard Malamud's *The Natural* (New York: Harcourt Brace, 1952; Farrar, Straus and Giroux, 1951), a first novel and, according to Roger Angell "our best baseball novel," is highly symbolic. Even the toughest, most realistic novels about baseball, such as Eliot Asinof's *Man on Spikes* (McGraw-Hill, 1955), while plausible and convincing, are for reading only, not research.

Books on Special Topics

The sources already listed cover most of the subjects that are of sufficient specialized interest to warrant a SABR committee — biographical research, bibliographical study, statistical analysis, ninteenth-century baseball. However, a few subjects have been slighted, and for those special topics — minor leagues, Negro leagues, and ballparks — it seems appropriate to include a brief list of basic books.

Minor Leagues

Two SABR publications were listed earlier: *Minor League Baseball Stars I* and *II* [48]. The following two books are also important to an understanding of the complex tapestry of the minors.

■ **71** Finch, Robert L., L.H. Addington, and Ben P. Morgan, *The Story of Minor League Baseball.* Columbus, OH: The National Association of Professional Baseball Leagues, 1953. 744 pp.

■ **72** Obojski, Robert, *Bush League: A History of Minor League Baseball.* New York: Macmillan, 1975. 418 pp.

Negro Leagues

More and more books are appearing on this once-neglected subject, but an enormous amount of research, some of it very difficult, remains to be done.

■ **73** Holway, John, *Voices from the Great Negro Baseball Leagues.* New York: Dodd, Mead, 1975. 363 pp.

■ **74** Peterson, Robert, *Only the Ball Was White.* Englewood Cliffs, NJ: Prentice-Hall, 1970. Reprinted 1984 by McGraw-Hill. 406 pp.

■ **75** Rogosin, Donn, *Invisible Men: Life in Baseball's Negro Leagues.* New York: Atheneum, 1983. 283 pp.

Ballparks

The SABR publication, *Green Cathedrals* [50] has already been listed. Here are two other basic books.

■ **76** Reidenbaugh, Lowell, *Take Me Out to the Ball Park*. St. Louis: The Sporting News, 1983. 288 pp.

■ **77** Shannon, Bill, and George Kalinsky, *The Ball Parks*. New York: Hawthorn, 1975. 276 pp.

Privately Published Books

Many good baseball books, especially ones of regional interest, are being published privately, some of them by SABR members. Although these books do not get the national publicity that major publishers provide, they are often valuable additions to your baseball library. Indeed, if they cover your specialty, they are indispensable.

■ **78** Overfield, Joseph M., *The 100 Seasons of Buffalo Baseball*. Kenmore, NY: Partners' Press, 1985. 252 pp.

   A comprehensive, first-rate history of the Buffalo Bisons, carefully researched, well-organized, capably designed, and nicely illustrated, this book should be studied by anyone thinking of self-publishing. Another excellent book of the same kind in an oversized format, also privately published, is James H. Bready's *The Home Team* [Baltimore], 1958, 1971, 1979.

■ **79** Beverage, Richard E., *The Angels — Los Angeles in the Pacific Coast League: 1919-1957*. Placentia, CA: The Deacon Press, 1981. 286 pp.

   Beverage's book is a straightforward, illustrated chronological history of the minor-league Angels. The author also produced a second PCL-team history under his Deacon Press imprint, *The Hollywood Stars — Baseball in Movieland: 1926-1957*. Both are admirable histories with appendices containing team and individual records.

■ **80** Crissey, Harrington E., Jr., *Teenagers, Graybeards, and 4-F's*. 2 vols. 1981, 1982. 150 pp., 179 pp.

Covering World War II baseball in the National and American Leagues, these books can be useful to researchers as source materials, since they consist entirely of first-person narratives based on transcriptions and correspondence. In the first volume, 40 National League ballplayers tell their stories of the war years. In the second volume, 43 American Leaguers do the same. All teams are represented.

Unpublished Sources

The variety of textual sources suitable for use in baseball research is staggering, and by no means all of the sources have been published. Some of them are just too esoteric to justify publication. There aren't enough people interested in the topic to warrant the expense of typesetting, printing, and binding. But for those few researchers who are interested in the subject, the unpublished source can be priceless. The difficulty lies in finding it.

Masters' Theses and Doctoral Dissertations

If you find a master's thesis, it will probably be by word of mouth: "Oh, yes, Joe Babcock over at Steerforth University did some research on ballplayers' salaries in the 1890s" — that kind of thing. Doctoral dissertations are easier to locate. An index called *Dissertation Abstracts International*, published by University Microfilms International, is an annual list (from 1861 to the present) that lists dissertations written at approximately 500 American and foreign colleges and universities. Subjects are indexed by key words. For twenty dollars or so, you can buy a print or microfiche copy of almost any of the dissertations listed. Or, less expensively, you can order a copy of the dissertation on interlibrary loan. (See page 23).

If you are doing research on baseball fiction and poetry, to take a single example, you might want to look at P.A. Knisley's dissertation, "Interior Diamond: Baseball in 20th Century American Poetry and Fiction" (Ph.D. dissertation, University of Colorado-Boulder, 1978). The more academic your topic, the more likely you are to find a dissertation on it. Graduate-level scholars are seldom interested in pondering the relevance of gee-whiz player stats and the like, at least not with a view toward climbing the academic ladder.

SABR Committee Materials

Obviously, you don't want to overlook completed or in-progress research in your own backyard. Some of SABR's work is incomplete. Some is tentative. In other words, not all the work done by SABR committees is readily available. But if you are doing research on the Southern Association, and half a dozen dedicated SABRites are poring over individual player records in that league, you should learn about it. By the same token, the committee chairman is virtually certain to know about individual, non-SABR-sponsored research that has been done on your topic. When I expressed an interest in the NYP-Eastern League, John Pardon, the Minor League Committee chairman, immediately gave me the name of Edmund Leonard, the recognized expert on the history of the league. Leonard's exhaustive research is his own, not SABR's, but the SABR lead proved invaluable. When I wanted the 1937 Elmira roster for my own research, all it took was a phone call.

Hidden Sources

This is the catchall. Somewhere out there, you can almost bet on it, there is more material on your area of special interest than you can now envision. You won't know what the material is until you find it. That may sound rather mystical, and as you progress in your research, you may begin to feel that it is. One source leads to another. One breakthrough brings a whole portfolio of unexpected riches.

Hidden sources can be anything, anywhere. No numbered list of books will direct you to them. Only persistence, coupled with a dash of luck, will yield the sources that nobody before you — absolutely nobody — has examined and used.

CHAPTER 4

Getting It Right

A great deal of misinformation about baseball has found its way into print. For a variety of reasons, even the most carefully compiled statistical lists can contain errors. The original source may have been wrong. The researcher may have introduced an error in copying down the information. Errors may have crept in during the process of publication. A fair percentage of the work of SABR researchers involves checking existing "factual" information and correcting it when wrong.

Adding to the confusion is the fact that baseball reporting in the early years, and even these days to some extent, is a curious combination of fact and fiction. The myths, legends, and lore of baseball are an intriguing part of the national pastime, but they can be troublesome to a researcher who is trying to sort truth from fantasy, which is something a researcher often has to do.

The Need for Accuracy

How oft we sigh
When histories charm to think that histories lie!

Thomas Moore, the Irish poet, wrote those lines more than 150 years ago. They are as true today as they were then. Some of the most appealing baseball books are rife with errors. When a writer caught up in his subject begins to deal with a multitude of facts — as baseball writers do — he should ideally check them out. But that doesn't always happen. Instead, the writer relies on memory, or myth, or his own reading of questionable accounts. Not surprisingly, the chances are good that his book will perpetuate old errors, introduce new ones, or both.

One principal job of a researcher is to get the facts rights. What is published in the *Baseball Research Journal* is, above all, supposed to be factually correct. This doesn't mean that it can't present controversial ideas, speculative comparisons, or personal reminiscences. The *Journal* features many such articles. For example, Bill Deane's "Players Today Better Than Oldtimers," *BRJ* 1985, is controversial. Bill Kross's "Is N.L. Really Better? Study Raises Doubts," *BRJ* 1984, is speculative. And Allen H. Quimby's "An Afternoon with Red Lucas," *BRJ* 1981, is a personal reminiscence.

But whatever the nature of the article, the facts contained in it should be accurate. Deane and Kross can't doctor the statistics (or get them wrong out of carelessness) on the way to proving their points. And Quimby, although he is reporting on a personal interview, can't write that Lucas "served up the Bambino's 712th home run on May 25" if in fact he didn't. The Quimby article is filled with names, dates, incidents, and statistics — all of which require checking. In other words, even if Red Lucas happened to remember something incorrectly, Quimby couldn't accept that faulty recollection and include it without qualification in the manuscript.

Factual accuracy is the responsibility of the researcher. Even if the editor of the piece is as widely knowledgeable as L. Robert Davids, Clifford Kachline, or John Thorn, he cannot be relied upon to catch — and should not be expected to check — every particle of fact (". . . Stan Musial's fourth straight walk came in the sixth inning of the May 14, 1944, game against Brooklyn's 18-year-old rookie Cal McLish . . ."). Every item in that factual string has to be right, and it's up to the researcher to see that each one *is* right.

Henry Ford said, "History is bunk," and Anatole France wrote that "the historical books which contain no lies are extremely tedious." A serious baseball researcher should accept neither of those statements. As many outstanding books and articles prove, good research can be both factually accurate and interestingly presented.

A Look at Secondary Sources

Baseball is a popular subject. It attracts a large number of enthusiastic writers and readers whose concern for factual precision is not paramount. Popularly written books and articles vary enormously in quality. Some of them are excellent, some are not so good. You have to determine which are which.

Nearly all the books you find in the 796.357 section of your public library are what are called secondary sources. A secondary source is a book or article that is not first-hand information, but is based on original material, on other secondary sources, or on both. By its very nature, a secondary source contains the author's judgments, inconsistences, and mistakes. Its quality depends upon its author. Sometimes secondary sources are excellent and can be used profitably in original research. Such sources are often helpful in providing a broad, readable overview of the subject.

Here are three questions to ask yourself when evaluating secondary sources:

1. What is the publication date of the book or article? In some cases, the most recent date may be the best; in others, it may not. If you want to know Kevin McReynolds' career stats through last year, you will need the most recent *Official Baseball Register*. (The 1983 *Register*, for example, will show his career stats only through Reno and Amarillo.) On the other hand, if you are doing research on Branch Rickey, you may find that a book written during Rickey's lifetime, such as Arthur Mann's *Branch Rickey: American in Action*, captures the events and mood of the day better than more recent books.

2. Who is the author? What is his expertise? In some ways, these two questions may seem unfair. After all, a book or an article should stand on its own. If it's good, it's good, and who cares about the author's credentials? That's a legitimate point as far as it goes, but it begs the question. If you are trying to evaluate the source, you need all the help you can get. You don't yet *know* the quality of the book or article. An awareness of the reputation of the author may be the next best thing. If the book or article was written by a respected baseball historian, you are probably safe in thinking you can rely on it, but you should remember that even the best authors can make mistakes. The dust jacket of a book, or a note at the bottom of the first or last page of an article, usually gives a brief sketch of the author.

3. What is your common-sense opinion of the source? Just by looking at a table of contents, a few paragraphs, some captions, and/or the index, you may be able to make a reasonable judgment about the quality of the source. If you wonder what reviewers thought of a recent book, you can look it up by author's name in the appropriate volume of *Book Review Digest* [4]. Usually the book will be reviewed in the same year as its date of copyright, but if you don't find it in that year's volume, try the next year's. Naturally, the deeper you get into any research topic, the easier it will be for you to evaluate sources on your own.

The Use of Primary Sources

Using a primary source means getting your information straight from the horse's mouth. If you have a filled-in scorecard from a game you attended years ago, the scorecard is a primary source for the events of that game. If you examine players' questionnaires at the National Baseball Library, you are using a primary source. If you check the box scores of every Nashville Vols game of 1936 in the Nashville *Tennessean*, you can consider the newspaper a primary source (although technically the official scorer's score-sheet, rather than the newspaper's box score, is the primary source for each game). If you interview a baseball figure from the past or present, your information comes from a first-hand observer and is a primary source.

Primary sources are what you want to use, if you can get them. If you rely wholly on secondary sources — on second-hand accounts — you will merely be reshaping existing research, not doing original research.

Still, you have to be wary even with primary sources. First-hand though they are, they are not always models of objective truth. Newspapers make mistakes. Books written by baseball players (or their named or unnamed ghosts) do not resemble holy writ. There are no perfect witnesses. Most people are poor observers. Liars and charlatans exist. How can you be sure that your facts are accurate, and, tougher yet, that your conclusions based on those facts are valid?

The simple answer is that you can't, at least not always. Nevertheless, there are degrees of credibility, and you will often have a sound, gut feeling of your own as to how much reliance you should place on a particular source. Beyond that, you can check one source against another, a topic that will be covered later.

If your primary source is a person you are interviewing, here are some pitfalls to watch out for:

- **Faulty memory.** Whether the interviewee is recalling an event last week or six decades ago, there is the ever-present possibility of his getting some of the facts wrong. Certain kinds of facts are easy enough to check. But it may be difficult or impossible to track down others. That presents you with a dilemma. Should you include the unverifiable facts in your book or article, or should you work around them? No unqualified answer is possible. It depends on the topic and the circumstances. If everything, or nearly everything, the interviewee told you checks out, there is a good likelihood that the uncheckable facts are true, too. If what was said turns out to be filled with mistakes, however, the unverifiable facts are a much greater gamble. In either case, the conscientious choice is to avoid including material about which you have doubts, or to include it with your expressed caveat to the reader.

- **Emotion.** No baseball player, manager, umpire, or owner is an impartial commentator on his own life and deeds. Everyone has likes, dislikes, biases, quirks, and blind spots. These may be artfully concealed in an interview, but they are usually present is some form. As a researcher, you should be on guard against statements that seem not to square with known facts. For example, if an aging interviewee suggests that a superstar from his era is vastly overrated, you will want to explore his reasons for saying so, but you will also want to keep in mind that he may have strong unexpressed reasons, emotional reasons, for his adverse judgment. In most cases, you don't have to be a psychologist to spot emotional factors at work in an interview.

- **Self-justification.** Even the most straightforward interviewee is likely to find persuasive reasons — ones not reflecting on him — as to why things sometimes went wrong. That is only human. It is human, too, for the researcher to want to go along with an interviewee's self-justification. Most interviews are pleasant encounters, which makes it doubly hard for a researcher to take sharp, retrospective issue with what was said. But it may be necessary. The person interviewed can rationalize all he wishes about his career; the researcher should not. A researcher, no matter what his admiration for the interviewee, is not a cheerleader but a truth-seeker. He is trying to sort out reality from recollections and occasional half-truths. Gaetano Salvemini, an Italian historian, put it well: "Impartiality is a dream and honesty a duty. We cannot be impartial, but we can be intellectually honest."

You Are the Judge

Research involves more than digging through a pile of indisputable facts and offering them up in organized form to readers. First of all, there *are* no indisputable facts, or very few. Most facts require assessment of some sort. Primary sources — the kind you will ordinarily use — demand appraisal. At best, they are likely to be a mixture of eyewitness and hearsay evidence. Therefore, in the end, research comes down to judgment. What will you accept? What will you reject? Viewed in those terms, research is a creative pursuit, an exercise in choice and discernment. You find facts and then verify them.

Jacques Barzun and Henry F. Graff in *The Modern Researcher*, fourth edition, point out that verification in research "relies on attention to detail, on common-sense reasoning, on a developed 'feel' for history and chronology, on familiarity with human behavior, and on ever-enlarging stores of information." In other words, a good researcher has most of the attributes of a good detective along with a keen sense of history.

Fact vs. Opinion

Contrary to textbook dogma, there is no clear dividing line between fact and opinion. It is a fact that Ty Cobb went 4-for-20 in the 1907 World Series. You can prove that statement to be true without difficulty. But it is also true that Ty Cobb was one of the greatest baseball players of all time. Although the previous sentence is stated in the form of an opinion, it is hardly one any longer. Ty Cobb's status in the baseball pantheon can surely be regarded as an accepted fact today. You don't have to go through the factual evidence yet another time to prove it.

On the other hand, if you were to say that Riggs Stephenson was one of the greatest ballplayers of all time, you would be stating an opinion. Knowledgeable fans would disagree. They would ask you for your evidence. You would have to marshal facts to support your opinion, starting no doubt with Stephenson's .336 lifetime batting average. This is the kind of opinion, by the way, that lends itself to research, and, if the case is persuasive enough (as it probably isn't with Stephenson), can result in a thought-provoking article based on facts. The key phrase is "based on facts." An opinion cannot be supported entirely with more opinions; for instance, "My brother and I saw Old Hoss Stephenson play at Wrigley Field during the '29 season, and believe me . . ."

But if opinion is slippery, so are facts. For years it was a "fact" that Walter Malmquist had the highest season batting average in minor league history — .477 for York in the Nebraska State League in 1913, according to official figures published in the annual Reach Guide. SABR researcher David Kemp decided that Malmquist's record should be documented. By conducting a box-score search in the York and Grand Island, Nebraska, newspapers, he established that Malmquist's .477 mark could not possibly be accurate, indeed that the available but incomplete box scores gave him only a .342 percentage. Kemp's research is described in detail in *Minor League Baseball Stars II*, "The Mysterious Malmquist," page 43.

Checking Facts

The best way to check the accuracy of a fact is the way Kemp did, to go back to the primary source — not to the Reach Guide, which contained the error, but to the individual box scores of York's games in 1913. As a general rule, newspaper box scores are the baseball statistician's main primary source.

Another way to check facts is by comparing sources. The difficulty with such a comparison, of course, is that all the sources you look at may have derived from the same inaccurate original source. You could have "proved" the correctness of Malmquist's .477 average by comparing the stats in the Reach Guide, the National Association's *The Story of Minor League Baseball*, and SABR's *Minor League Baseball Stars I*. Since all three of those respected sources base their information on a statistical error made by the Nebraska State League and then perpetuated by Reach, they all agree — and all are wrong.

Comparisons are a useful starting point, though, and they may lead to the truth. One kind of factual comparison that is always desirable is the proofreader's kind — a careful comparison between your notes (or photocopies) and your own final manuscript. Mistakes are frequently made in transcription or in typing. There is quite a difference between a .309 batting average and a .390 batting average, but a typist can raise or lower percentages like that in one careless moment.

And then there is the matter of common sense, something you should always apply when you come across eye-popping figures, remarks, or events. David Kemp must have had the shadow of a doubt about Malmquist's hitting .477. You would probably have a similar doubt if you saw Tim Raines credited with a .390 batting average for 1984. You might not know offhand that the correct mark is .309, but you would surely be inspired to check.

When stories and anecdotes are at issue, rather than facts and figures, the same general principles apply. In the 1986 *Baseball Research Journal*, James Tackach's article "Hazards and Tips for Researchers" offers this advice: "When confronted with several versions of the same story in baseball histories, accept the version of the story by the writer who acknowledges sources and presents and resolves conflicting views of the same event." That goes back once again to the reliability of sources. Impartial primary sources are best, but reasoned evaluations by later historians can be valuable, too.

When facts are in question or when sources disagree, consider these three criteria:

- **Proximity.** A newspaper reporter commenting on a play he observed that very day is likely to be more reliable than a writer interpreting the play 50 years later. The reporter had the considerable advantage of closeness in time and space.

- **Competence.** Some reporters are more skilled than others. Some historians are more capable and conscientious than others. Writers don't carry around gold badges proclaiming their competence, but time and thought should enable you to reach your own conclusions as to who is trustworthy and who isn't.

- **Objectivity.** A person with an ax to grind is not an ideal source. What you want is a source that has nothing to gain or lose by telling the truth. A lack of objectivity can affect autobiographies ("What will posterity think?") and can also taint biographies ("Jazz it up a little, Jim.")

The Thrill of a Successful Quest

SABR researcher William F. Gustafson, writing in the *1973 Baseball Research Journal,* used those words — "the thrill of a successful quest" — to describe the rewards he found in his efforts to unearth biographical data on obscure major league players.

Along the way, Gustafson and a few other researchers have written helpful articles about their efforts. Veteran SABR members will have read these articles, but since the articles provide vivid case studies of baseball research, a brief review is in order.

Gustafson, William F., "Locating the Old-Time Players," *Baseball Research Journal,* 1973, pp. 40-45.

This article gives a brief, annotated rundown of the kinds of sources Gustafson used in searching for biographical data on baseball players. Included are reference books, death records, newspapers, directories and compilations, telephone directories, city directories, address lists, clubs and fraternal organizations, genealogies, government organizations, teammates, and neighbors. Certain annotations contain anecdotal illustrations of the uses Gustafson made of the sources he describes.

Haber, Bill, "A Favorite Paige of Mine," *Baseball Research Journal,* 1977, pp. 90-94.

Haber explains in detail his search for the vital statistics of George Paige, a righthanded pitcher who appeared in two games with the Cleveland Americans in 1911. From the Chief of Police in Jackson, Michigan, to a supposed neighbor of Paige's, to a local historian in Paw Paw, Michigan, to the Indiana State Prison — and on and on — Haber notes the steps that led him at last to the home of the ex-ballplayer's son and to the information he was seeking.

Schmidt, Ray, "The Betts and the Brightest," *The National Pastime*, Winter 1985, pp. 10-12.

This is the story of Bill Haber and Clifford Kachline's quest for information on a pitcher or pitchers named Betts — Harold and/or Fred — who had appeared in only two major league games separated by a decade. Like the Haber piece described above, Schmidt's article explains exactly how Haber and Kachline went about solving their mystery. The author names the sources they used and tells of their successes and failures en route to finding the one true (Harold) Betts.

Tackach, James, "Hazards and Tips for Researchers," *Baseball Research Journal*, 1986, pp. 86-88.

Focusing on a single incident, the suspension of pitcher Charles Sweeney of the Providence Grays in late July 1884, Tackach presents three separate versions of the incident, then explains how he himself decided to handle it for an article in *The New York Times*. Tackach concludes by giving four research strategies and tips drawn in part from his experience with the Sweeney incident.

CHAPTER 5

A Picture Is Worth a Thousand . . .

Many research projects gain an added dimension with the inclusion of pictures. Among SABR's most popular publications are *The National Pastime* pictorial issues, which are virtually all pictures with accompanying captions. Even statistical studies, such as SABR's *Great Hitting Pitchers,* are enlivened by a few well-chosen photos. There is no denying the appeal of visual images in baseball publications, whether books, newspapers, magazines, or journals.

The question is, how do you go about getting pictures? While it may be fairly easy to find biographical information on a player from the 1920s, it can sometimes be very tough to find a photo of him. Textual material tends to be carefully indexed and painstakingly cross-referenced. There are bibliographies of bibliographies. But pictures are seldom so neatly catalogued, and the search for the right one can be a Sherlockian puzzle.

This chapter covers just the basics.

Kinds of Pictures

Photographs are primary, of course. The history of baseball coincides with the history of photography. In 1839, the same year that Abner Doubleday was allegedly creating the modern game of baseball at Cooperstown, New York, Louis Daguerre was announcing his own invention, the daguerrotype, to the French Academy of Sciences. Small wonder that when you think of baseball illustrations you think of photographs. With rare exceptions (as when doing research on baseball cards, perhaps) photographs will be the main object of your search.

The other kinds of illustrations are familiar enough, though less commonly used: paintings, postcards, drawings, cartoons, indeed all the items that librarians call ephemera — newspaper advertisements, posters, cigar labels, and other promotional materials. A glance through the pictorial issues of *The National Pastime* or at Daniel Okrent and Harris Lewine's *The Ultimate Baseball Book* (Boston: Houghton Mifflin, 1979) will indicate the range of materials possible. Ephemera are often a part of individual or institutional baseball collections, but, as you might expect, they are almost never indexed or cataloged.

What to Look For

As always, the specific nature of the project will determine what you need in the way of illustrations. Nevertheless, there are a couple of useful guidelines to keep in mind.

Avoid the old familiar pictures. The easiest photo to get may be the photo you have seen a hundred times before. Unfortunately, so have many of your prospective readers. If possible, find something new, or at least something that many of your readers will not have seen before. This may mean a longer, harder search, but it's usually worth it. If your subject itself is relatively unfamiliar — Civil War baseball, let's say — then any pictures you find are likely to be new to your audience. In that case, it comes down to a matter of choosing the best from among those you find.

Make sure you get a reproducible picture. In doing textual research, you will probably come across a lot of pictures you can't use. Photos from microfilm will not reproduce satisfactorily. Photos from newspaper or magazine clippings will yield very poor reproductions. In general, you should avoid any photo that has previously been screened for halftone reproduction. What you want is a black-and-white glossy print made directly from an original negative, or, barring that, a print made from the copy negative of a properly rephotographed original print. (An original print is one processed from the original photographer's negative). Line drawings in black and white will always reproduce satisfactorily. Even a clear photocopy of a line drawing will sometimes reproduce well, although you may find it necessary to use white-out to perfect the copy.

Three Ways to Get Photos

One obvious way to obtain a photograph is to order it from an institution that collects photos — a library, a museum, a historical society, a commercial photo agency. There will be a fee in nearly all cases, varying from the modest amounts charged by the Library of Congress or the National Baseball Library to rather sizable amounts, particularly for color, charged by stock photo agencies such as the Bettmann Archive, UPI, Culver Pictures, or Sports Illustrated Pictures. The minimum fee you are likely to pay is ten dollars, while the maximum can soar into the hundreds. Clearly, this method of obtaining prints can be a luxury, one that is generally unaffordable by amateur researchers.

If you are ordering photos by mail, you can save a good deal of time as well as needless correspondence by asking at the outset for a photocopy or photocopies of the best available print or prints on your subject. Some institutions, such as the Minneapolis Public Library, will send you one or more photocopies in response to your first inquiry, but many will not. It pays to make a direct request. When you do so, offer in your first letter to pay for the cost of photocopying, an expense you can expect to be billed for in any case.

A second method of obtaining pictures is by searching on your own. Instead of asking for a specific photo or kind of photo, you can visit the collecting institution and go through its files. Nearly all institutions provide a service for supplying reproducible prints. Again, there will be a fee, but it will usually be lower than the mail-order fee and considerably lower than one charged by a stock photo agency. If you search through private collections, you may have to obtain prints on your own. A local photographer or photography store will probably be able to help you, but once again there will be a fee for the work. If you can photograph prints yourself, thus obtaining a good copy negative, you can save time, money, and the necessity of borrowing the original print from the owner. The catch is that successful copy photography requires both proper equipment and skill. A single-lens reflex camera, a copystand, and balanced lights are the essentials. A poorly photographed print will yield an unusable copy negative, often because of uneven lighting or problems with focus or exposure. Even the best copy negative will give you a print of slightly lower quality than the original.

Photography on your own — not merely copy photography — is the third way of obtaining pictures. A capable photographer with good equipment will find this method useful in virtually any kind of research. If you are interviewing an old-time ballplayer, you can photograph the person himself. You can photograph memorabilia items. If you are doing ballpark research, you can photograph ballparks that are still standing, whether they are in use or not. Any print you obtain in this way should be a reproducible one of near-professional quality, not a blurry snapshot.

Where to Begin

If you are a first-time picture researcher, you will find that a good place to begin is with an illustrated book on your subject. Check the picture credits, which may be in the front or back of the book, or on the pages where the individual pictures appear. This approch will give you a point of departure, because you know that the sources listed have at least some pictures of the kind you are seeking.

If your project is a regional one — baseball in Cleveland, say — start your picture research in that area. Work from the specific, or local, to the more general, or national. Begin with the Cleveland Public Library, which has a sizable photo collection as well as a picture collection relating specifically to Cleveland. Even if the Cleveland Public Library doesn't have what you need, someone there may be able to direct you to a probable source, perhaps the Western Reserve Historical Society, or the Ohio State University Library, or a private collection.

Mark Rucker, co-editor with John Thorn on *The National Pastime* pictorial issues and other projects, believes that finding such helpful leads — "One out of every two people you ask will suggest another possible source" — is the most important single factor in picture research. Once your research starts, it can expand rapidly and productively through this kind of networking. The more you zero in on the exact material you need, the more knowledgeable the advice will become, because people who specialize in a topic are likely to know others who specialize in the same topic. The public library in a large city is a particularly good place to start, because librarians frequently know who some of the specialists are.

Along this same line, consider asking the chairman of the relevant SABR committee for help. For example, if you are researching the Cleveland Buckeyes of the Negro American League, you would be remiss not to ask the chairman of SABR's Negro Leagues Committee for advice on picture sources.

If your subject involves a small city (Glens Falls, New York, let's say), you might want to check the ZIP Code listing in the back of the most recent SABR Membership Directory (12801 for Glens Falls) to see if any members live there or in a nearby community. If the answer is yes, you may find it useful to ask one or more persons by phone or letter if they know of any potential picture sources in the area. Like any other approach, this may or may not work, but it is often worth a try.

In general, keep these principles in mind:

Figure out in advance where the pictures you need are likely to be. If you are looking for photos of Donie Bush, for example, it's obviously significant that Bush spent nearly his entire playing career (1908 to 1921) with the Detroit Tigers. You will also want to note that Bush managed for three seasons each in Pittsburgh and Chicago and one each in Washington and Cincinnati. Possibly relevant, too, is the fact that Bush was born and died in Indianapolis. It's true that all of this information may be more than you need to know, or need to consider, if you have decided at the outset, for example, that the one photo you want is at the National Baseball Library. The point is that a researcher living in Texas, say, will probably *not* start his search for photos of Donie Bush at the Galveston Public Library. He will start either (a) with a place where a large and varied collection of baseball photos exists, or (b) with the places where Donie Bush played, managed, or lived.

Explore all possibilities. This advice on picture research is the same as that on textual research. If the Detroit Public Library can offer no help on Donie Bush, don't give up. Library help at long distance is chancy at best. The staff is often busy with local requests. A search is required for photos, and a faraway researcher is unlikely to get priority treatment. But somewhere there are photos of Donie Bush, probably a good many of them, and it will pay you to keep searching. Use your imagination. If the obvious sources all fail, you may come up with a long shot that works.

Photo Directories and Collections

A number of directories of picture sources exist, but none of them are especially helpful for baseball. You will do better simply to look through lists of picture credits in books or magazines that deal with your subject. Once you know some of the commercial sources, you may want to get in touch with them, in which case the latest issue of *Literary Market Place (LMP)* will be useful. All libraries have it. Under the heading "Stock Photo Agencies," you will find more than a hundred agencies and their addresses listed. Another section in *LMP* lists photographers, many of whom maintain stock files of their own photos.

If you want to check library collections, you will find a complete list of American and Canadian libraries in the latest edition of *American Library Directory*, a two-volume resource published (like *LMP*) by R.R. Bowker Company. Since this directory lists staff and special collections, it can help you in your research and may lead you to a specific person to contact for pictures.

The outstanding collection of baseball photos in the United States is unquestionably that of the National Baseball Hall of Fame and National Baseball Library (see page 25). Many other libraries have useful collections, but except for the Library of Congress (see page 26) most of these collections have a regional emphasis. Among the libraries frequently cited as photo sources are the New York Public Library, the Boston Public Library, and the Chicago Historical Society (pre-1925 baseball). Any public library or historical society in your area of regional interest is worth checking. Many of the photographs for Ronald A. Mayer's well-illustrated *The 1937 Newark Bears: A Baseball Legend* came from the Newark Public Library, while the Buffalo & Erie County Historical Society supplied Joseph M. Overfield with a number of key photos for *The 100 Seasons of Buffalo Baseball* [78].

Tracking Down Sources

Photographs, like gold, are where you find them. Some sources that would seem to offer a rich vein often don't. Newspapers and professional baseball clubs, for instance, may prove to be dead ends. Both generate a lot of good pictures, but neither is in the business of supplying them to historical reseachers. You may find a happy exception, but on the whole there is not much profit in pursuing these sources.

Individuals, on the other hand, whether news photographers or ex-professional ballplayers, can be very good sources. They aren't usually in the business of supplying pictures to historical researchers either, but they may be willing and able to do so. Photographers are likely to have the negatives, which is a plus. Ex-players, along with ex-managers and front-office personnel, will often have some original prints that you (or a professional photographer or studio) can copy.

Your best bet for finding out about photographers is by word of mouth, although you may be lucky enough to find one you need listed on a photo credits page. If you are looking for photos of individual, living ex-players, you can check *The Sport Americana Baseball Address List* [21] and proceed from there. Of course, the photos you receive in this way are generally intended for fans and autograph seekers and will not be original prints, which means they may not be reproducible. If the player owns an original print, you may be able to make an arrangement to get a copy, but at long distance (regardless of your offer to pay all copying costs and postage) that may be more of an imposition than you or he will want to consider.

There are many private collectors of baseball pictures and memorabilia. If your interest is regional, you can probably find out about one or more of them from a local library or historical society. Nationally, you will sometimes find the names of private collectors listed in the photo credits in a book or magazine. In that case you may have to do some searching to find out where the collector lives. SABR may well be able to help, through its Executive Director or Publications Director.

Do the searching that is necessary. Don't give up your quest for pictures too easily. Be persistent in the face of disappointments. A good picture can add a great deal to your baseball research project. Indeed, the right picture, when it is finally found, may be one of your research coups. It may even be the major one — the most original contribution of all.

Credit Where Credit Is Due

Stock photo agencies and most libraries and historical societies will state the conditions under which you may use a picture. Most photo suppliers have variable rate schedules for reproduction rights. Generally, nonprofit use (as for a SABR publication) will be less expensive than profit-making use (as for a commercially published book). This is particularly true when the supplier itself is a nonprofit organization — a library or historical society, for instance. But the rates and conditions for reproducing a picture for a commercial publication may vary, too. For instance, you may be able to use the picture in a book or magazine but not in advertising. You will probably be restricted to one-time use, which means you cannot copy the print and then use it again at your convenience. Most organizations will ask that you credit them in the publication in which the photo appears. A few will insist that the credit line be printed on the same page as the photo, but most will accept a consolidated page-reference listing, one including all pictures, in the front or back of the book or magazine.

Individuals may or may not make their preferences known in regard to credit. As a rule, it pays to supply a credit line for every source, not just because courtesy to the lender dictates it, but also because one or more of your readers may want to obtain the same picture. If you have used lists of photo credits as a starting point in your own research, you will appreciate the value of such lists to other researchers. Naturally, the policy of your publisher will play a major part in determining how picture credits are handled. Some publishers insist on them. Other publishers are much more casual about it. If printed credit is required by the terms of your agreement with the supplier, you will have to be sure it is given.

CHAPTER 6
Going Public

Research does not always involve writing for publication. Some researchers prefer to gather the information — statistics, for example — and then have someone else present their findings to the public. The presentation may be oral, as at a regional or national convention, or it may be written.

This chapter assumes that you want to present your research as a published article or book. The suggested guidelines will be basic ones, appropriate to SABR publications, general interest periodicals, and most baseball books. Since SABR does not require footnotes or bibliographies, those topics are not covered in any detail. A writer who intends to publish in scholarly journals, or with an academic book publisher such as Greenwood Press, is probably already familiar with the kinds of documentation required. If not, many good references are available.

Before You Write

It makes sense to find out early whether there is any editorial interest in your topic. A letter or a phone call to the editor of the *Baseball Research Journal* or *The National Pastime* will give you a preliminary reaction to your idea for an article. The editor won't be able to give you a flat "Yes" on speculation, but he may be able to give you a flat "No." Here are a few of the common reasons for a negative response:

Someone has already covered the topic. An article on your topic is either in print now or is scheduled for publication in the near future. See Dan Rappoport's "Six Phases of a Baseball Research Project" on the next page.

Six Phases of a Baseball Research Project

1. ENTHUSIASM

2. DESPERATION

Where's *The Sporting News* or *The New York Times?*
I've been to thirteen libraries and none of them carry
issues from 1898.

3. HOPE

There's a librarian who knows what a balk is.

4. DELIVERANCE

She knows where the source of the material I need is
hiding, and it is at her fingertips!

5. JUBILATION

The material needed for the project has been found.
The report is written.
The report is submitted to the *Baseball Research Journal*
or *The National Pastime* for publication.

6. DISILLUSIONMENT

The subject matter has already been covered in a
previous *Baseball Research Journal* or *The National
Pastime*. This article is merely an update of someone
else's research.

— Dan Rappoport

The topic is of too limited interest. While it may be a matter of family
pride that your Uncle George played second base for the James-
town Falcons in 1952, his PONY League experiences probably
won't be broadly appealing enough for an article. It's true that any
subject can be made interesting, but there's no need to start out in
this deep a hole.

The topic needs to be focused. "A Comprehensive History of the Los Angeles Angels" is too broad a topic for an article. It might make a good book. (In fact, it has made a good book, SABR member Richard E. Beverage's *The Angels: Los Angeles in the Pacific Coast League, 1919-1957*, published by The Deacon Press [79].) More appropriate for a brief article is W.R. Schroeder's "The 1934 Los Angeles Angels" in the *1977 Baseball Research Journal*.

From Source to Finish

If you have avoided the foregoing pitfalls and the editor has said he would like to take a look at the finished manuscript, you have passed the first hurdle. You can begin work in earnest, assembling the information you need to write the piece. The next step after that is to get your material into shape for submission.

Working from Notes

The notes you take will depend on the nature of your project, its length, and the publication for which you are writing. Most academic researchers use 3x5 cards as bibliography cards, putting the needed information about each source on a separate card. If your final book or article will have neither footnotes nor a bibliography, you may decide that bibliography cards are unnecessary. Remember, though, that an editor may require fact-checking on your part, and, in that event, you will find it very difficult to check if you have kept no information about your sources.

Your notes go on other, larger cards, usually 4x6 or 5x8. Bibliography and note cards can be carried and stored in expansion wallets or in cardboard or metal boxes. If you use both bibliography and note cards, fill out the bibliography card first. That way you will avoid the problem of having a note in your files and its source in a library far away — and no clue as to the details of the source.

The great advantage of cards over other forms of notes is that they can be shuffled to match your outline (see page 12). If your outline changes — as it almost certainly will during the course of research — you can rearrange your notes to fit the revised plan.

If your research is statistical and will lead to tables rather than text, you will still need an organizing plan to keep your notes straight. As a rule, you will find that either chronological order or alphabetical order is a logical choice.

Working from Photocopies

Note-taking is a lot easier than it used to be. At one time there was no choice but to write out all your notes in longhand. Today you can usually photocopy pages from a book or magazine in even the smallest library. In larger libraries that have sophisticated equipment, you can also copy pages from microfilmed sources directly off the microfilm reader. Photocopiers generally have a coin slot that requires the payment of 10 or 15 cents for each page copied. If you make a great many copies at one time, you can often have the librarian lock the machine open with a key and pay for the entire batch of copies when you finish.

Photocopies have the twin virtues of speed and accuracy. You cannot miscopy with a photocopier. However, you can go astray in other ways. If, while the copier light is on, you move the item you are copying, you can get fuzzy, unreadable printing. You can lose the edges of a page through misplacement or by trying to copy pages from a book that will not lie flat.

Most frustrating of all, you can easily forget to keep track of the sources from which you are copying. Unless you remember to write on each photocopy the name of the book, magazine, or other periodical you are copying from, along with any other important information, you are almost certain to end up with a few usable notes and no clue whatever as to where they originated. Make it a habit to write source information on all photocopies while you still have the source in front of you.

Sometimes you may want to make later written notes from your photocopies. At other times, you may find that it is easier and faster to refer directly to the photocopies when writing.

Working from Audio or Video Tapes

Oral history, and, increasingly, visual history are becoming important tools for the researcher. The tape recorder and now the videocassette recorder have made it possible for researchers to obtain primary source material in a way that was unimaginable in the earlier days of baseball. Lawrence S. Ritter's *The Glory of Their Times* [58] is the nonpareil baseball book based on interviews. But there are others (for example, Harrington E. Crissey, Jr.'s, self-published *Teenagers, Graybeards and 4-F's*, vols. 1 and 2 [80]); and many recent books make use of taped interviews along with other sources.

Videotape cassettes and movie film can bring past events vividly to life. Anyone doing research that involves, say, the 1975 World Series would do well to refresh his memory by renting and viewing the film on that series available through the National Baseball Library.

A VCR owner has the equipment to do tapings of games himself, while the owner of a camcorder can videotape interviews, old ballparks, or anything else that will further his research.

How best to use these various audiovisual resources is pretty much up to the individual researcher. It pays to transcribe audio tapes, if you can, because otherwise the search for a needed quote or anecdote can be extremely time-consuming. Perhaps the best way to use film and video materials is simply to take notes in the time-honored way.

It seems safe to say that researchers of the future will rely more and more on primary-source audiovisual materials in writing baseball books and articles. It seems equally clear that the new technologies will spur an increasing number of researchers to develop their own AV productions.

Working from a Variety of Sources

Only rarely will an article or book be based on a single kind of source. More often the sources will be mixed. Here is a list of sources I used in writing an article on minor league slugger Joe Munson, the only player in Eastern League history to bat .400 for a season. Munson is included in SABR's *Minor League Baseball Stars II*, but this article was written prior to that book's publication. [Note: The kind of source is listed in brackets after each entry. Note, too, that this list — minus the bracketed items — can be used as a model bibliography if you are writing for a publication that requires a bibliography.]

"'Babe Ruth' of Western." Omaha, NE: *Bee-News*, August 23, 1928. [*newspaper clipping*]

Carlson, Joseph M. (Joe Munson). Personal interview and tapes, Upper Darby, PA, March 28, 1981. [*personal interview, audio tapes, memorabilia*]

Dailey, Larry. "Joe Bats .515 in Brilliant Achievement." Tulsa, OK: *Evening World*, August 18, 1927. [*newspaper clipping*]

Eddleton, Oscar. "Under the Lights." *Baseball Research Journal*, 1980. Cooperstown, NY: Society for American Baseball Research, 1980. [*SABR publication*]

Keyes, Ray, ed. *Silver Anniversary: Eastern League Record Book.* Williamsport, PA: Eastern League, 1947. [*league publication*]

Lutz, Dick. "Keeping in Touch: Munson's Record Homer." Harrisburg, PA: *Telegraph*, August 30, 1925. [*newspaper on microfilm*]

"Nine Baseball Pennants Won by Harrisburg." Article in Harrisburg Senators' program of 1946, furnished by Marie H. Redus, Curator, The Historical Society of Dauphin County, July 7, 1981. [*from query letter*]

O'Donnell, Harry. "Homers Few in NYP Loop; Munson Good." Elmira, NY: *Star-Gazette*, May 21, 1937. [*newspaper clipping*]

Patriot, The. Harrisburg, PA: May 5, 1925, through September 12, 1925. [*newspaper on microfilm*]

Reichler, Joseph L. ed. *The Baseball Encyclopedia.* 4th ed. New York: Macmillan Publishing Co., Inc., 1979. [*general reference*]

Taylor, Sec. "That Munson Guy!" Des Moines, IA: *The Des Moines Register*, August 12, 1929. [*newspaper clipping*]

Length, Format, and Quotations

The length of a manuscript is determined by its topic and its intended mode of publication. Most periodicals have guidelines for length that are either explicit or implicit. By looking through the *Baseball Research Journal* and *The National Pastime*, you can easily determine the average length of articles. In general, a new contributor should stay within this range, or perhaps aim short.

As for format, the standards are nearly universal: double-spaced typewritten pages with approximately one-inch margins on all sides. With pica (10-point) type, this will give you about 250 words on each page. With elite (12-point type), you will get roughly 275 words per page. These figures are useful to know, because they make it unnecessary for you to count the actual number of words on each page.

Although this book does not deal at length with manuscript form, there is one aspect of the subject worth noting: quotations. Quotations are tricky. There are dozens of rules for them. However, if you keep one basic point in mind, that words enclosed in quotation marks are the *exact words of the speaker*, you will avoid the most common pitfalls. For instance, you will not write a sentence like this:

McQuinn, when asked about his .201 average with the Reds, conceded that "he was not a pull hitter."

That can't be right. If the sentence is an indirect quotation, as it seems to be, it should have no quotation marks at all. If it is a direct quotation, it can be punctuated in various ways. Here are two:

McQuinn, when asked about his .201 average with the Reds, conceded, "I am not a pull hitter."

or

McQuinn, when asked about his .201 average with the Reds, conceded that he is "not a pull hitter."

Notice that these quotations assume that McQuinn was asked about his .201 average — and that the article was written — while McQuinn was still an active player. If the question had been asked him after his retirement, the quoted *am* and the unquoted *is* would both have to be *was*. To punctuate a quotation correctly, think about the speaker's exact words and consider the time when they were spoken.

SABR publications have no footnotes. Typically they don't have bibliographies either, although Philip J. Lowry's *Green Cathedrals* [50], a 1986 SABR special publication, has one. For readers who would like to learn more about formal manuscript style, specific writing techniques, or self-publishing options at greater length, three useful references are listed at the end of this chapter.

Using a Critic Reader

Before submitting your manuscript to a prospective publisher, have someone else read it. This may be someone in your family, although unless that person is knowledgeable about baseball, you may get better feedback from a SABR member. Here are some questions to ask the critic reader to keep in mind:

- Will the topic appeal to informed baseball fans?
- Is the title of the paper appropriate and, if possible, catchy?
- Does the manuscript make its main points clearly?
- Does it contain any obvious errors of fact?

- Does its organization help keep the reader on track?
- Does the manuscript end effectively?

Remember that even the most severe critic reader may be reluctant to open fire on you with both barrels. Even if you tell him or her that you want absolute honesty, you may not get it. But, as every editor will tell you, there is another problem inherent in this kind of once-over-lightly reading. A manuscript often looks better to a reader at first sight than it does to an editor in the throes of blue-penciling it line by line. Editing is picky work; reading is not.

The very best critic reader, in the last analysis, will be you. Put the manuscript aside for awhile. Then read it slowly and appraisingly. Read it as if another person, error-prone and none too brilliant, had written it. Be your own toughest reviewer. After spending a week or two away from the manuscript, you will be amazed at how much you find to correct and improve.

Submitting the Manuscript

When you are convinced that the manuscript represents your best effort, write a brief covering note to the editor and get two 9x12 manila envelopes. One of the envelopes is to be self-addressed, stamped, folded in half, and included in the package you send to the editor. It will help if you have a postal scale to determine the return postage needed. Although Ring Lardner once said that a return envelope offers too great a temptation to the editor, the fact is that you should include one. Without it, a far greater temptation for the editor is to throw your manuscript in the wastebasket. (I once had the owner of a small press donate my unsolicited manuscript to a local historical society, from which the editor told me I could retrieve it by sending a dollar for postage.)

Allow plenty of time for the editor to make a decision. You have sent out only one manuscript, but the editor may be deluged with submissions. Or he may be in the middle of a rush project. Or he may want to have other people read it. Or . . . In any case, don't be discouraged if it takes a month or two for a decision to be made — or for an annual publication, longer. Conversely, don't be unduly encouraged just because the manuscript has been held so long. The best attitude to take toward a manuscript submission is that you will hear its fate when you hear its fate. With luck (well, not really luck) the answer will be "Yes," and you can look forward happily to the day when you will see your contribution in print.

The Self-Publishing Option

SABR publishes very few book-length manuscripts. If you intend to write such a manuscript, or have written one, you may decide to do what a number of SABR members have already done — publish it yourself. Of course, if your subject has a large potential audience, you will want to try to attract the attention of a major publisher. But if the appeal of the potential book is regional or otherwise limited, your best bet may be self-publishing.

Besides avoiding the hassle of trying to interest a major publisher in a nonblockbuster, there are a couple of other good reasons:

1. You keep control of your book. Major publishers usually have their own ideas about title, content, typographic design, copyediting, jacket design, promotion, and so on. That may not bother you in the least, but then again it may. After all, it's your book. You probably have at least some thoughts on how it should be handled. And if you handle it yourself, and do the job right, the published book can look every bit as good as it would if a major publisher had produced it. Or possibly better. Witness SABR member Joseph M. Overfield's handsome, self-published *The 100 Seasons of Buffalo Baseball* [78].

2. Self-publishing can be good business. Not only does self-publishing offer you very real tax advantages, it also gives you a higher percentage of the money realized from the sale of your book. Now, it's true that 50% of nothing is nothing, as major publishers often point out when defending their 5% to 10% royalty rates. But it's also true that a self-publisher is more likely to promote his book enthusiastically than a big publisher is. You have a personal, continuing interest in it. With a regional book, you are also likely to know the market better — and be able to deal with it on a more personal basis — than a distant publisher does.

Some people think there is a stigma attached to self-publishing. Nonsense. These people are thinking of vanity publishing — paying someone else to publish your book — a practice that has a deservedly bad reputation. Self-publishing, on the other hand, has always been respectable. The list of well-known self-publishers includes a galaxy of literary figures: Stephen Crane, Edgar Allan Poe, Carl Sandburg, Mark Twain, Walt Whitman, and dozens of others whose names are renowned today.

But self-publishing is no cinch. You have to be not only the writer but also the editor, designer, and promoter of the book. There is plenty to learn, and you shouldn't jump in without doing some research on the topic and perhaps talking with some self-publishers.

The Collaborative Option

Much of this handbook has dealt with individual efforts directed toward publication, and you may have gotten the idea that the only aim of research is a book or article under your own name. In fact, a great deal of SABR research is done collaboratively, as a glance at the list of credits in publications such as *Minor League Baseball Stars I* and *II* [48] and *Great Hitting Pitchers* [49] will show. SABR committees encourage and often initiate team projects. There is plenty of research to be done by nonwriters. A number of committee chairmen (not to mention some editors at commercial publishing firms) are looking for help. They will welcome you even if your interest in writing narrative history is nil.

On the other hand, if you do want to publish under your own name but lack the writing skills to get into print, you may find a member of SABR who is willing to join with you in a shared effort. A main purpose of the organization is to foster cooperative work. The membership directory, issued annually, "encourages members to exchange information and assist each other in research projects." The ZIP Code listing at the end of the directory facilitates finding potential assistance in the geographical area of your interest.

For More Information

This chapter has admittedly left a lot of ground uncovered. In a book on baseball research, there seems to be no real need to cover the whole field of writing, editing, and publishing. Other books cover these areas very well. The following three deserve special notice.

Felt, Thomas E., *Researching, Writing, and Publishing Local History.* 2nd ed. Nashville: American Association for State and Local History, 1981. 166 pp.

Felt's book is a brief, practical guide aimed at intelligent amateur historians, with a strong emphasis, as the title indicates, on the sources and techniques relevant to local history. It is an excellent down-to-earth introduction to basic research, manuscript preparation, and book and periodical production.

Poynter, Dan, *The Self-Publishing Manual.* 3rd ed. Santa Barbara: Para Press, 1984. 352 pp.

Here is an author who practices what he preaches. Dan Poynter is said to run the largest one-person book publishing company in the United States. His manual deals with every aspect of self-publishing: writing, starting a publishing company, printing, promoting, pricing, selling, and distributing. Don't be put off by the IBM Selectric type in which Poynter's text is set. The book, filled with facts, hints, and illustrations, is a valuable treatise on self-publishing.

Sabin, William A., *The Gregg Reference Manual.* 6th ed. New York: Gregg Division/McGraw-Hill Book Company, 1985. 421 pp.

This is a concise, well-organized guide to punctuation, spelling, usage, manuscript form, letter writing, footnotes, bibliographies, and, indeed, virtually every problem that is likely to occur in ordinary written communication. It is less complete than the frequently recommended University of Chicago's *Chicago Manual of Style,* 13th ed., or Prentice-Hall's *Words into Type,* 3rd ed. However, it is also less cumbersome and easier to use than either of those references.

Index

Page numbers in **boldface** are references to main entries in the Checklist of Sources, Chapter 3

A

C

E

F

O

S

U

V

W

X

Y

Z

A000015154965